MOON OVER SASOVA

Published by Hellgate Press
(An imprint of L&R Publishing, LLC)
Hellgate Press
PO Box 3531
Ashland, OR 97520
email: sales@hellgatepress.com

Interior Design: L. Redding

Cover Design: Edward Noriega is a Cooper Union graduate who currently serves as Director of the Design Center at Troy University, and is also a professor of Graphic Design in the Art and Design Department at Troy.

ISBN: 978-1-954163-17-1

Printed and bound in the United States of America
First edition 10 9 8 7 6 5 4 3 2 1

MOON OVER SASOVA:

One American's Experience Teaching in Post-Cold War Slovakia

Christopher Shaffer

Hellgate Press Ashland, Oregon

For my wife, Amber, who has listened to my stories about Slovakia far more than anyone should have to, and my mother, Jane Shaffer Elliott, for introducing me to travel in Europe, thus ensuring that I would forever be in debt.

CONTENTS

INTRODUCTION

A Sign on a Pole

I OWE MY SLOVAKIA EXPERIENCE largely to serendipity. As I neared the end of Spring Quarter at Auburn University in 1991, I needed eight elective credit hours to graduate. I had taken two years of German, and at the prodding of my favorite professor, Dr. Tom Nadar, I signed up for the University's study abroad program in Mannheim, Germany. It was worth ten credit hours, and it cost only $300 more to spend the summer in Germany as opposed to Auburn. As a side note, Auburn happens to be one of the hottest places imaginable during the summer months; thus, two months in Germany seemed like a good plan. It would also allow me to declare German as my minor, and practice my language skills in a real-world setting.

When I arrived in Germany, *Frommer's Guide* in hand, I was ready to study some, but travel more. We had afternoons and weekends free. Afternoons found me exploring towns near Mannheim; everyone in the program got free travel on area transit, so long as the destination was within a sixty-kilometer radius of the city. On weekends I picked farther off places to visit. One of those weekends I decided to go to Prague. I knew very little about the city, but having lived the first nineteen years of my life under the construct that was the Cold War, I was curious to see a city that had been behind the Iron Curtain, and everyone I talked to seemed to think it was the most beautiful and charming city they had ever visited. Prague had largely escaped damage during both World Wars, which added authenticity and original charm to its beauty. Some cities, such as Warsaw, Poland were so devastated during World War II that they can seemed hollow, bland recreations of their former glorious selves.

Another student in the program and I made the train trip to what was then Czechoslovakia on a Friday night. Neither of us knew what to expect, and we were both surprised at the green countryside. Everything I thought I knew from the evening news about the Eastern Bloc portrayed the place as grey and drab with no shortage of what I like to call Stalinist Towers throughout the region. We were surprised that a large percentage of the country is protected as national forest, which made for some beautiful scenery. Another surprise came at the border between Germany and Czechoslovakia. This excursion was not like the weekend trip to France a week prior. Czechoslovak soldiers with assault rifles strapped to their shoulders boarded the train when we arrived at the border. Everyone in the compartments was ordered out into the corridor, while everything was searched. After about forty-five minutes we were back on our way, but it was clear that the transition from an authoritarian to a free society would not be happening overnight.

Walking out of the main train station, the first thing I encountered was a stand selling hamburgers and Pepsi. Both items seemed somewhat out of context. The burger as it turned out was made of ground pork, which wasn't much of a surprise.

Pepsi being available was somewhat more of a surprise. Going forward, I noticed that Pepsi was everywhere, but Coca Cola was nowhere to be found. I would later learn that Pepsi was one of the first soft drink companies allowed into the former Soviet Union. In another twist, the Ruble was not an exportable currency, so the good people at Pepsico had to figure out how to get their profits back to the United States. Ultimately, they began exporting Stolichnaya vodka from the USSR to the U.S., allowing them to turn a profit in dollars.

Prague was more beautiful than I could have ever imagined. The architecture can best be described as Gothic on steroids. With only a day and a half to see the city, I made a commitment to myself to return to Prague after my studies were complete. I was already planning a two-week Eurail trip with my friend David after the semester. In the meantime, I took advantage of as many of the sites as possible, and that night discovered something that I decided was a budget traveler's best friend—goulash. Goulash soup at its best is prepared Hungarian style with a lot of paprika. The meat can vary—beef, pork, and venison seemed to be the most common choices. To this is added potatoes, beef broth, and tomato sauce. Served with dumplings it makes a hearty meal. It also tastes wonderful, fills the stomach, and is cheap. Plus, because it is so spicy, it is a great excuse to drink a few of the world's best beers. If there was a negative to ordering goulash, it was the perpetual look of disappointment that the request would leave on waiters' faces. Generally, an American entering a restaurant in Eastern Europe leads to expectations of a lot of money being spent. The waiters were always saddened to realize I was a student on a budget and would be ordering the cheapest thing on the menu!

I only saw the highlights of Prague during this visit. Walking from the train station, I quickly found myself at the top of Wenceslas Square and in front of the National Museum, a gigantic neo-renaissance building. Wenceslas Square is the Prague version of the Champs-Elysee, and not that long ago had been filled with Czechs who successfully called for an end to communism in their country. Walking away from the museum and down the square there are several narrow streets that lead to the Old Town (*Stare Mesto*). The Old Town is where several architectural gems reside, perhaps most notably the astronomical clock tower where crowds gather a little before the beginning of each hour to watch a mechanical skeleton ring the bells while a rotation of saints make appearances. Across the square from the clock tower is the Gothic-styled church Our Lady before Tyn, with its towering spires. Continuing onward one comes to the Charles Bridge, which leads to Castle Hill (*Hradcany*) and St. Vitus Cathedral.

As I explored, I was amazed at the feeling of optimism that seemed to be omnipresent. Vaclav Havel had just been elected president, and it seemed everywhere I looked there were signs with his photograph and a caption that read *Havel na Hrad* (Havel to the castle), the president's residence. However, the dichotomy of lingering totalitarianism amid newly found freedoms was everywhere. Access to the Charles Bridge was hampered by a busy street. Pedestrian access was limited by a traffic light that definitely favored keeping automobile traffic flowing over allowing the many people who were on foot to cross. Tourists—most of them Western—began jaywalking when they felt they could make it across the street in spite of the traffic. Largely unnoticed were soldiers standing on an island in the street's center. Suddenly, one of them lowered his rifle and pointed it at the crowd. All of us hopped backward onto the sidewalk.

Once across the street, it was possible to access the pedestrian-only Charles Bridge that stretched across the Vltava River, and then lead to the base of Castle Hill. On the bridge, lined with statues of a myriad of saints on both sides, a variety of vendors were selling art, jewelry, and small puppets. I would later find out that Prague was known for its puppet makers. Also, on the bridge—much to my surprise—were quite a few people smoking marijuana, something that was still illegal in Czechoslovakia. No one seemed to be particularly worried about the police doing anything to them; I rarely saw a policeman on the bridge, and I don't remember ever seeing a soldier. To this day, I am not clear on how law enforcement was so obsessed with jaywalking, but not particularly concerned with individuals flagrantly flaunting their drug laws. In the name of full disclosure, I have always believed marijuana should be legal, I just had no interest in being shot by a Czechoslovak soldier, or experiencing what life was like in one of their prisons.

The far side of the Charles Bridge gives way to the base of Castle Hill. As I made the climb upward, I would frequently turn around so I could get increasingly better panoramic views of the city. This journey culminates with St. Vitus Cathedral, an architectural wonder that is Gothic to the max, complete with gargoyles, spires, flying buttresses, and beautiful stained glass, most notably the art nouveau series of panels by Alphonse Mucha.

As planned, I stayed on in Europe at the conclusion of my studies. The choice was to return home for graduation, or spend two weeks riding the rails. After mulling this conundrum for at least five seconds, I decided to stay. I bought a second-hand (technically third-hand) Eurail pass for twenty-five Marks. I was told that after the passes were initiated, conductors rarely checked the holder's passport. If the story that was related to me was true, the original owner, Warren W. of Ontario, Canada (to whom I am forever grateful), lost his ninety-day Flexipass on about day eighty-eight or so of his travels. Out of money, he went to a Eurail office in Italy for assistance. In the confusion, they ended up issuing him a brand new pass. At this point, he had free train rides, but no funds for food or places to sleep. Since there was no way for him to continue his travels, he sold it to a mutual acquaintance, who then passed it on to me. Anytime I think about the expense of travel, I try to remember that I did travel by train for free for two weeks in 1991.

David and I visited our German professor, Tom, and two of his friends in Bonn before heading to Munich; then to Venice where I treated myself to a birthday present of Jack Daniels and Coke on the Piazza San Marco. Celebrating age twenty-one with a drink in Venice seemed the most sophisticated thing any human could ever do. Vienna was next, and where we split up, and I traveled onward to Prague.

I did learn one piece of valuable information on the train ride from Venice to Vienna. Trains in Europe will sometimes separate on long trips, and the two parts will then go to completely different destinations. David and I were actually supposed to be traveling to Salzburg rather than Vienna. In the middle of the night I woke up, and for whatever reason, something felt wrong. I stopped a conductor, and in my weak German, I tried to figure out if we were headed to the correct destination.

"*Enschuldegung, bitte,*" I stammered. "*Wann kommen wir nach Salzburg*?"

He looked perplexed, and said, "*Salzburg*? *Wir fahren nicht nach Salzburg.*"

Not sure what to say, I replied, "*Wo the fuck fahren wir*?"

And that is the story of how I got to see Vienna for the first time. We stayed in a youth hostel, and the next day I put David, not the fan of backpacking in Europe that he expected to be, on a train back to Mannheim, where he would recuperate for a few days before we both reconnected and flew home out of Frankfurt. That afternoon, I would continue onward to Prague, after exploring some of the beautiful Viennese sights.

On the train trip to Prague I learned something new: traveling alone can be a good thing. You meet people. It just happens naturally. If you are with someone else, or a group, you focus on each other. Conversely, other people feel they are interrupting a couple or group by engaging with them, but are comfortable starting a conversation with a solo traveler. I found myself in a compartment with three other people. Each spoke a different language, but all of us spoke one language in common with at least one other person. We talked for a couple of hours, with each of us translating for the others as necessary until two of the passengers reached their towns, which left me and the gentleman across from me alone in the compartment on the way to Prague. His name was Milan.

When the train stopped at the Czech border, he looked at me and said, "*Ich habe hunger, und sie haben hunger*" (I am hungry and you are hungry). He got off and then returned shortly with an apple, a bag of pretzels, and a beer for each of us.

He looked at me and said, "*Ein Geschenk aus mein Herz, und die Herzen von die Tschechoslovaki Leute*" (a present from my heart and the hearts of the Czechoslovak people).

We continued to talk, and as we were pulling into the main train station in Prague, he asked me where I was staying. When I told him that for the first night I was going to stay in the train station, he was horrified, and said that due to crime in the station, that could not be an option. We walked to the state travel agency, Cedok, and arranged for me to rent an apartment for a few nights. Then, worried I would not be able to follow the directions, he walked me from the train station, and down the grand boulevard that is Wenceslas Square. The apartment was off a side street about halfway down the square. He made sure I was safely inside before dashing off to catch the last subway of the night home. This was my first introduction to Czechoslovak hospitality, and it would definitely not be the last.

I spent three nights in Prague before returning to Germany to catch a flight back to the United States. While walking to a restaurant one night I noticed a flyer posted on a telephone pole, an ad looking for Americans to come teach in Czechoslovakia, with telephone numbers that could be torn off. I ripped one off and tucked it in my book bag, thinking to myself, *You never know*. I then hurried onward for a heart healthy meal of goulash, dumplings, and beer in a cellar restaurant that I had come to like on Wenceslas Square. A much fancier sister restaurant inhabited the upstairs, but I preferred the downstairs prices. I also preferred eating with the Proletariat. It was more touristy upstairs, and the people in the more modestly priced restaurant seemed more authentically local.

When I got home, I found the telephone number, and called it. At the time, I hadn't noticed, but it was an Alabama area code. I had literally traveled to Czechoslovakia from Alabama to find an ad by Alabamians asking for people to come to Czechoslovakia! The odds of that happening certainly seemed slim, and, though I had never been a particular fan of John Calvin, it also made the whole affair seem quite predestined. The group recruiting teachers was named Education for Democracy (EFD). It was founded by a Canadian soldier, Major John Hasek. Ann Gardner, from the University of South Alabama, partnered with the Czechoslovak government to run that part of the organization.

Before I could go anywhere to teach, I needed to complete

my certification. My BA is in history, and job opportunities were scarce. I received a letter in October 1992 from EFD indicating they had accepted my application, and I completed my studies in December. On January 14, 1993, I found myself headed to a new country, as the Slovaks had officially given the Czechs their ring back two weeks prior in what came to be known as the Velvet Divorce.

1

Disentanglements

THERE WERE A FEW OBSTACLES in my path as I prepared to leave the country. During my final quarter in school as I worked toward completing my teacher certification, I met a young woman and we began dating. It was an unexpected and pleasant surprise. My plane ticket was purchased though, and I was headed to Slovakia. For almost a year, I had been focused on making this adventure a reality. It also made a difference (in my mind) that the adventure was temporary, and that I would be coming back to "the real world" in six months. In my twenty-two-year-old head, everything made perfectly logical sense. I would take a brief break from the relationship and go to Slovakia. During my stay in Slovakia, we would both be completely faithful to one another, and then a half-year later, everything would return to normal. Amazingly, things largely worked out as I had hoped. About three months after I returned from Slovakia we resumed seeing each other.

On the family front, everyone had been supportive of my little adventure. This included my grandmother, who was in her mid-eighties. I had expected her to resist the idea of my going to some far off place by myself, but she was surprisingly supportive. In December, I found out that she had been bluffing. She called me with a multitude of grave concerns.

"Christopher," she said, "I have been reading a lot about Czechoslovakia."

"It is actually about to be Slovakia," I replied.

"I know. They are having a revolution!" she exclaimed.

"No they are not," I explained. "They just have decided to go their separate ways. There has been no fighting."

Trying another tack, she said, "They're Communists!"

I persisted with my current events lesson, "No they are not. They just got rid of the Communists."

"If you won't go, I will pay you back for your plane ticket, and give you an extra $1,000," she offered.

Capitalist that I am, I did pause for a second before declining. "This is important to me, and I really want to go. I think it will be good for me, an adventure, and I may never again have a chance to do something like this."

All that the poor woman had left was a Hail Mary pass. "Christopher, do you realize that a lot of the streets over there are cobblestone? Do you realize what that could do to your feet? I admit that I had not considered the podiatry-related implications of this journey. Ultimately of course, I decided to live life on the edge, and go anyway.

My grandmother was one of several faithful letter writers who corresponded with me while I lived in Slovakia. It is funny how different communication is today. Without email and cell phones, receiving mail elicited excitement on the level created by Corporal Radar O'Reilly on *M*A*S*H* when he would deliver letters to the doctors. I would receive—almost weekly—a letter from my grandmother on onion-skinned paper in a lightweight envelope used for airmail. She might have resisted my leaving, but once the decision was final, she became one of my most ardent supporters. There were advantages to not having these modern-day communications devices though. It forced independence and meant that I would not be able to fall back on my known world back home. Instead, I had to fully get out of my comfort zone and explore and meet people; which is the point of any immersion experience. Upon reflection, there was so much more depth in the letters I wrote and received while in Slovakia than in the emailed communication of today that in a weird way I may have been better tuned into my friends and families lives than if I had had today's modern conveniences.

2

EFD Orientation

I SET A PERSONAL RECORD on the trip to Stupova, Slovakia, where the EFD orientation took place. I was awake for thirty-one straight hours traveling. The flight out of Atlanta was smooth but cramped. The good news though, was that I had pleasant people around me, including a sixteen-year-old exchange student from Bremen, Germany named Miriam. Miriam's story demonstrated some of the things that could go wrong when people move to other countries. She had signed up for a year's exchange program in the United States but had an unpleasant time with her host family. She had hoped to see as much of the United States as possible, but got to go nowhere, and was largely ignored by the family. Consequently, she was returning to Germany a half year early. In hindsight, I have wondered if there was some cultural misunderstanding involved in her experience. Over the years while backpacking in Europe, I have found it commonplace to meet young teenagers who are traveling together and staying in youth hostels. Americans, on the other hand, rarely would give a child that age so much freedom. Either way, I was sorry she had such a bad experience, and hoped I would fare far better on my own adventure. We landed in Frankfurt with no problems.

During a layover in Frankfurt, I started talking with a man named Jim, who was en route to Moscow, as part of a group named Friendship Force, a non-profit organization with a mission to improve intercultural relations. It still exists today. Jim and I had an immediate rapport, and we started talking about where we had been and where we hoped to one day go. He started traveling late in life. Never having been out of the country, he called Delta on a whim when he was forty-five years old and asked how much it would cost to go to Mexico. He never looked back and had been on the move ever since. He asked me if I wanted to have a beer, and when I said that it was 9:00 a.m., he pointed out that we were in Germany, where the societal rules governing beer consumption were not that strict. We drank and talked for two hours, celebrating out arrival in Europe, after which I caught my connecting flight to Vienna, Austria.

In Vienna I was immediately met by representatives from EFD, and we waited for the rest of the new English teachers to arrive. Once we had all assembled, it only took about an hour to reach our destination of Stupova, Slovakia. En route, we went through Bratislava, which many would quickly start referring to as Blava. I had heard that it was a depressing city to see, and it lived up to my minimalistic expectations. Much of the historic old town was destroyed in the name of progress; a major highway was constructed. Only a few city blocks of Bratislava's former glory were preserved. We were also introduced—mercifully in passing—to the largest housing development in Slovakia, which was named Petrzalka. Every building was exactly the same height and color, and the development just went on as far as our eyes could see. At one point I was told that Petrzalka had the highest suicide rate of any group of apartment blocks in Europe. I never have found out if that was true or not, but if there were ever a contest for such a thing, I can understand why they might be competitive.

Our hotel in Stupova was nice by the standards of any country. I had been unsure of what to expect. That night I started meeting some of the other English teachers, or lectors as the Slovaks would call us. One of them, Merrill, who was from Denver, Colorado, overheard where I was from and asked me if it was true that everyone from Alabama was inbred? *Nice guy*, I thought to myself. Merrill and I, as well as five other people, were all being placed in a town named Banska Bystrica.

The next morning several of us went to see what would be the first of many castles visited while in Slovakia. Pajstun Castle is actually a ruin of the original built in the 13th century and destroyed by fire 500 years later. It was a steep walk to the top, but the views were spectacular once there. Slovaks love what they refer to as "the nature," and venues such as Pajstun Castle are popular with young and old alike, although not necessarily in January. Even as cold as it was that day, it was a good way to get an introduction as to how old Slovakia's culture was compared to my relatively young United States.

One of the more interesting aspects of our group was its age diversity. The majority of us were fresh out of college, but then there were people who were retired, or just taking a year off. Gloria was a feisty sixty-seven-year-old with a short haircut. We started talking while walking around the castle ruins, and came back down the hill together. Gloria was in front, and I was behind her. The first stretch going downhill was particularly steep, and she slipped and fell. In a flash I wondered how I would get this elderly woman down the mountainside. Almost before I could process the thought, Gloria hopped back up and said she was fine.

"How did you get up so quickly?" I asked, realizing that I would have probably taken more time to collect myself than she did.

Gloria's reply was direct, "When you decide to do something like this at my age, you want everyone to be able to see that you really can do it."

I could tell that Gloria was a bit of a bad ass. I knew immediately that I liked her, and would want to spend more time talking to her in the coming months.

I finished the night in the hotel bar and wrote in my journal about my adventures to that point. In the background was Barry Manilow's *Could It Be Magic* set to disco music. The bar had a disco ball, and I would come to learn that the Slovaks loved disco music. Over the course of the next half year, I would develop a theory that at the close of the 1970s every disco ball in the United States was boxed and sent to Slovakia. The ubiquitous disco ball could be found in almost every bar I went to over the next half year.

Dinner that night had been odd, I thought. Instead of Slovak fare, the hotel served something that was similar to an Indian dish. It tasted a bit off, but I was hungry, and apparently not very smart. As a result, in a few hours I got to experience food poisoning and its effects. The vomiting and diarrhea lasted for 30 hours. About ten other people were taken ill, and apparently the rest had iron stomachs. The next evening, I was able to go downstairs for about an hour and see people at the party that was taking place our final night in Stupova. The following day we would all be scattered to the Slovak winds and taken to the various towns that would be our new homes.

3

Pan Biel

MONDAY MORNING, FEELING BETTER YET weak, I headed to the lobby of the hotel to meet the people who would be driving me to Banska Bystrica. Once downstairs I found out that I would be sharing a flat with Merrill. We quickly put questions of inbreeding aside and became good friends. Besides, it was us against the Commies! I will point out now, that in hindsight I believe we were both lucky to become roommates. Although I do believe in the value of traveling alone, this situation wasn't travel, but rather a long-term living situation. It was good to be able to have someone to compare notes with, give and receive encouragement and advice, and also just speak English with. Merrill also turned out to have a remarkably high language factor, which was very useful. He quickly developed a functional knowledge of the language, and by the end of his stay he was almost fluent in Slovak. I would end up relying on my three years of German, which was commonly spoken as a second language by the Slovaks, as well as by developing a vocabulary of what I considered essential Slovak words that I spoke with a hybrid Alabamian/John Wayne accent. Although my Southern tongue never could quite wrap itself around spoken Slovak, my "essential vocabulary" theory worked reasonably well. The Slovaks tend to rely on a relatively small set of words, so if a visitor can learn the words for numbers, colors, foods and drinks, key phrases and greetings, he can get by fairly effectively. It probably also helped that it was a good time to be an American in Eastern Europe. We were still a mystery to the Slovaks, and almost everyone was eager to meet us and to be helpful.

We were met by Pan (Mr.) Biel, whose apartment we would be renting in a suburb of Banska Bystrica named Sasova. He was an older man, short, bald, with round glasses and a kind face. Accompanying him were his son and daughter. The five of us would soon get to know each other well. All of us, plus Merrill's and my luggage were crammed into an early 1970s Fiat Uno that would take us on the three-and-a-half-hour trip. Before leaving Bratislava though, we went to Mr. Biel's other daughter's house for an early lunch. It was good and involved lots of potatoes (*zemiacky*). We would quickly learn that we were now residing in a nation of people that loved their carbs.

The trip actually took six hours. The temperatures were well below freezing. The roads were icy, and it was snowing. I am from a place where if snow is predicted the entire state shuts down, so this was a new experience. Early in the journey we happened upon the aftermath of what must have been a horrific bus accident. The body of the vehicle was singed all over, and part of the roof looked as though it had been ripped off. Merrill and I shared a look that indicated we both had concerns about surviving this ride.

Every ten minutes or so, the Fiat would die. Sometimes we

got lucky and Pan Biel could coast to the side of the road. Other times, we all got out and pushed while Pan Biel steered. Once safely off the road, Pan Biel popped the hood, and dried off a bunch of cables. The car would start again, and we continued moving at a snail's pace through the tundra. South of Banska Bystrica, I kept noticing this bizarre looking land mass. I still don't know quite how to describe it, but it was similar to a field with oddly shaped formations coming out of it. I asked Mr. Biel's daughter, Claudia, what it was. She replied, "Is River Hron." I had just seen my first frozen river. This place was cold.

We arrived at our new dwelling cramped and ready to stand. Sasova was a development of perhaps seventy-five identical blocks of flats. They were as dingy on the outside as the current weather. Our address was Tatranska 5, and we were on the fifth floor of that building. We went up in the tiny elevator in three waves. As we started to go inside the apartment, we were immediately stopped by Pan Biel, who mimed that we were to take off our shoes. It is a logical thing to do in a country where the outside is covered in slush for a large percentage of the year, but I never did get entirely used to the custom. When visiting people, not unlike in Japanese homes, they almost always have sandals in some sort of a cubby that guests can wear.

The flat was minimalistic, but the heat worked. There were two bedrooms, separated by a hallway, a den with two chairs and a coffee table, a kitchen without a refrigerator, a bathroom that also housed the most bizarrely primitive clothes washer I have ever seen, and a separate room for a toilet. It always seemed so strange to have people say, "Where is your toilet?" Americans are invariably so delicate about this question. We always call it a restroom, as though we are excusing ourselves to take a nap. The beds were about three-quarters the size of an American twin bed, but they were firm and comfortable. The kitchen was minimally stocked with one large pot, a few forks, knives, and spoons, plates, cups, and mugs (four of each), and a corkscrew with a bottle opener (no doubt a Slovak kitchen essential). For the next six months, this would be home.

4

Home Sweet Tenement

SASOVA WAS SORT OF PETRZALKA lite. It was not as vast as Bratislava's housing development, but it was as grim. In the mornings when people were getting ready to go to work, and in the evenings when they returned home, grey skies turned brown, as residents turned up their coal powered heating systems. Brown skies turned to blue with the arrival of warmer weather and the blessed end of a need for radiators.

Rolling hills and mountains surrounding Sasova were beautiful features about where we lived, our frequent escape once warmer weather arrived. Everything in Sasova was identical. Each building looked the same. Between buildings every set of playground equipment looked the same. It reminded me of the scene in Madeleine L'Engle's *A Wrinkle in Time* in which children came out of identical houses at the same time each day and bounced identical balls for a set amount of time before returning inside. I feared that if I left our apartment, I would never be able to find it again. Consequently, I did not leave the apartment for the first day of my new life in my very new and strange settings.

Merrill went to the *potraviny* (grocery store) on our first full day in Sasova. He returned with basic supplies: *mlieko* (milk), *maslo* (butter), *chlieb* (bread), *pivo* (beer), and two kilos of *hovadzie* (beef). First, going to the grocery store is a great way to start learning a language. Second, I was curious how we ended up with so much beef.

Merrill explained: "I didn't know how to communicate, so I pointed at the beef, and when the butcher said what I figured was 'how much?' I held up two fingers. I meant two pieces, but I didn't know how to explain that he was giving me more than I wanted."

We had now largely blown our food budget for the month. To make it more fun, there was much about food in Slovakia that Merrill and I would both come to appreciate, if not love. Beef, though, was something that did not fall into the "love" category. It was unbelievably tough, and no matter what we did to it, it remained that way.

Once we had perishables in the apartment, another issue arose—how to keep food from spoiling without a refrigerator. I am not sure which one of us thought of the solution, but we realized nature could solve our problem. For the next three months, the balcony would serve as our refrigerator/freezer, though more freezer than refrigerator. Each morning, we got up an extra hour early to bring the milk and butter in to thaw. While waiting, we listened to the BBC news, one of the few ways we could receive news from the West. Occasionally we bought a copy of the *International Herald Tribune*, but with our salaries at about $100 per month each, we quickly learned we had plenty of money to live on as long as we bought Slovak goods (yay state-imposed price controls!), but Western goods cost what they were actually worth, or in different terms, they cost what they cost in the West.

Price controls were an odd concept for a couple of good capitalists to wrap our heads around. Under communism, the state mandated what everything would cost. As a result, everyone making a Slovak wage, which would only last a few days in the West, would allow a person to survive, albeit without many luxuries. The State also had a not very well-hidden agenda, which was to foster the alcohol addiction that existed throughout the country by keeping the price of alcohol—particularly beer—low. A liter of beer cost about 10SK (Slovak Crowns), whereas a liter of milk, cost 15SK. Which of these refreshing beverages was the State encouraging its population to purchase?

The next day it was my turn to venture out. Merrill gave me directions to the store he found, and off I went with my book bag. We needed a few more basic supplies as we began stocking the kitchen. When I arrived at the store, I was quickly stopped by an imposing and grim woman. It took a minute to figure out what was happening. There were a finite number of shopping carts and customers could not shop until a cart became free. Even if you wanted something as simple as one can of Coca Cola, you could not enter the store without a cart. As a result, everyone got to line up two different times, first for the privilege of shopping, and second for the privilege of paying. I never completely understood the logic of this system. The grocery stores were small, so it may have been devised for reasons of practicality. However, this was a barely post-Communist society, and from what I could tell, the Communist Party seemed to really like lines, and after about fifty years, the Slovaks got used to standing in them.

I do believe that the persistent lines and the never-ending bureaucracy served a purpose on the part of the prior Communist regime in Slovakia. All of these annoying facets of their society had a way of occupying peoples' time to the point that it gradually wore them down and made them less likely to question the state's authority. People slogged through the system in the same way they slogged through the slush produced by the Slovak winter. You just tried to get through to where you were going, and surviving the ordeal was enough.

I waited a few minutes and watched a young woman pay for her groceries. She came to where I was standing, unloaded her cart, looked at me and said neutrally, "*Nech sa paci*," which means "there you go." It is one of the most common phrases in Slovak. The grocery store consisted of only a few aisles. Sometimes I think we have too many choices in the United States. Abundance of choice was definitely not an issue in Slovakia. There was one of everything. There was one cereal—Knusper Flakes—with the jovial Knusper bunny on the front of the box. We would look at him daily as we waited for our milk to thaw. There was also one brand of laundry detergent, unfortunately named Colon. Whenever we would wash clothes for the next half year, it was impossible to resist pulling a shirt out of our primitive washing machine and saying, "There is nothing like the fresh smell of colon!"

As I had feared, after leaving the potraviny, I immediately got lost. Snow had turned to slush, making walking miserable. Everything seemed to be a dingy grey—the ground I was trudging; the buildings I passed, the sky overhead. After about two hours, I got my bearings, and was able to find Tatranska 5. I never got lost in Sasova again though. A truism I have learned over the years traveling is that one of the best things you can do to orient yourself is to get lost in a new place. Once you find your way to where you are going, you will be unlikely to get lost again.

5

First Day on the Job

I HAVE ALWAYS HAD A fascination with the Cold War era. I went to Saint Paul's, a Catholic elementary school in Birmingham, Alabama, during the 1970s, and the nuns stressed the evilness of the Communist system. I never had to cope with the useless, yet certainly terrifying duck and cover drills children had to go through only a few years prior, but the nuns made it clear that the Soviets wanted us dead. I can remember being about eight years old and sitting with my mother at the kitchen table asking her to explain to me why the Soviets wanted to kill us. Eleven years later, I can remember opening presents on Christmas Day as Nicolae Ceausescu and his wife were executed live (so to speak) on CNN. I also read two newspapers per day and focused on the international sections. Add Tom Clancy's and Martin Cruz Smith's books to this mix, and it quickly becomes clear that this was an obsession. It shouldn't be a surprise that I had trouble containing my excitement when I found out that I would be working on one of the upper floors of the former Communist Party headquarters for central Slovakia, and my employer would be the Statne Jazykova Skola (State Language School). Welcome to the wonderful world of teaching, Comrade.

I worked in a fifteen-story 1960's era building; its design best summed up as brutalist architecture. Once inside, I was taken to meet the principal, who looked like the classical "Russian Bear" of a Communist bureaucrat. He was quite pleasant from what I could tell. We had to communicate through a translator.

He looked at me and said, "Vodka ... cognac?"

After all, it was 8:00 a.m. In the end, it was one of each. I am six feet tall, and weighed 120 pounds at that time, having always had trouble gaining weight. I could tell that I was going to need to watch myself in my new surroundings. With that said, suddenly the Siberian winter did not seem to bother me nearly as much. My salary was also explained to me. As with all other transactions in Slovakia, I would be paid in cash. My salary was 3,000SK per month, which was essentially the equivalent of $100 per month. I would be paid every two weeks in 1,500SK increments.

I worked with five classes primarily. Two groups were mine exclusively, and I taught them four mornings per week. The other group was another teacher's class; my role was to assist. The teacher's name was Maja (Maria), and she also served as my mentor teacher. Her students met in the evenings. My classes were third year students who were able to speak at the conversational level. The evening students ranged in age from seven to their seventies, and were primarily at an intermediate level with their studies. After our first class Maja invited me to have a glass of wine with her at Caffe Copia, a *vinaren* (wine bar) down the street from the school. It was there that I got to discover how surprisingly good Slovak wine is, particularly the reds. To be clear, the French don't have to worry about any competition, but it does taste good, and at the equivalent of one dollar per liter, it is a great value if nothing else. Copia would quickly become a post-evening class tradition. Sometimes several students would accompany us for a drink and to practice their English, and sometimes we went alone. Over time we formed a remarkable bond, and Maja played a large role in helping me develop an understanding of Slovakia and its people.

6

Josef and Lucy and Josef

EARLY IN OUR STAY, WE met Josef and Lucy and their son Josef in the elevator coming home from work. They lived on the seventh floor of our apartment block. Josef was impeccably dressed. Slovaks tended to dress quite casually for work. Jeans and an open collar shirt were quite acceptable. It was rare to see someone with a starched shirt and a tie. They invited us to come upstairs for a drink later that evening.

Two hours later we entered a much nicer version of our own apartment. The furniture was a vast improvement over ours. Josef had altered the entryway so that it had an arch, which gave a distinct personality to an apartment that was essentially like every other one in Sasova. There were also a lot of Western products around the place, including the liquor, which was not particularly easy to source at that point in Slovakia. Josef would later tell us about the one store in Banska Bystrica that specialized in Western goods. Slovaks as a rule did not shop there because they could not afford it. Once the Americans discovered the store (all told there were about twenty of us living Banska Bystrica at that point), I was fascinated by the one item they all wanted: peanut butter. Apparently when Americans are traveling in foreign lands that is the one flavor from home they crave the most. The Slovaks had no concept of it, and it could not be found in any of the stores except that one, and then only sporadically.

Josef was Serbian and Lucy was Croatian, which considering the war that was developing to our south, was an odd combination. He would occasionally give her verbal jabs about her ethnicity that were right on the borderline between rough and tumble humor and outright derogatory. They had immigrated to Canada in the 1970s where he made a small fortune in construction. In the late 1980s, he decided they should move back to then-Yugoslavia so they could be near family. After only a couple of years, Tito—the long-time Yugoslavian dictator—died, the republics began seceding along ethnic lines, and a civil war had begun. In addition to moving his family to Yugoslavia, Josef had also moved his money into Yugoslav banks. Once fighting broke out, the banks froze their clients' assets and only allowed meager monthly withdrawals in order to prevent a run on financial institutions across the war zone. Fearing that he would be drafted, Josef took his wife and son and left, but in an effort to stay close to their money and property they settled in Slovakia.

Josef was charming, but he perpetually had money-making schemes for which he tried to involve Merrill and me. Neither one of us could quite understand why he thought two twenty-two-year-old recent college graduates would have enough disposable income lying around to start a business venture, but apparently we looked rich. Our favorite idea came a few weeks later as we drank a beer with him in his apartment.

Josef looked at us from his chair and earnestly said, “Guys, I have a sure-fire investment opportunity. I had a potential partner, but he turned out—excuse me for saying it—to be a son-o-mom-beetch. I have been spending some time in the Czech Republic. They have the most amazing jams there. We could buy these jams, and we could sell them all over America. When you go home in a few months you could help me distribute these jams and we will all be rich.”

I said, “Josef, without even getting into what a land of abundance America is, we already have a lot of jam over there.”

The conversation went on for a few minutes and we realized finally that he was saying gems. Either way, we never got into the gem or jam business.

7

Private Tutoring

IT WAS COMMON FOR AMERICANS living in Slovakia to be asked to teach privately in addition to their regular jobs. It was a good way to make a little bit of extra money, hopefully help someone improve their English-speaking skills, while also gaining some more insight into the people and culture of Slovakia.

I would have two such jobs. The first came to me by way of Lucy, who introduced me to Susan and Samuel. Their boy, also named Samuel, was eight years old, and they wanted him to learn English from scratch. Samuel was a handsome boy with blonde hair and pale blue eyes. He loved playing soccer, and attended a sports-geared elementary school, as opposed to a traditional one. He had a bright and happy personality, and the only English he seemed to know was how to say, "Chrees, I am jester." He was a true beginner. I had no experience teaching children so young, and the only type of English I had expected to teach was at the conversational level. It was also fairly clear to me that I was not going to be able to avoid taking the job. Slovaks have an impressive way of passively applying pressure when they want something. Essentially the argument becomes, "I understand that you don't feel you can take this job, but just know you are all that stands between my son being a successful businessman or a low-level factory worker."

We settled on 70SK per lesson, and three lessons per week. That was the equivalent of 7% of my regular salary. On top of that, Susan looked at me, and was clearly evaluating my weight. She then said she wanted me to tutor Samuel around lunchtime, and she would make me lunch before each lesson. Next, she invited to Sunday dinner for as long as I was living in Banska Bystrica. I didn't meet another *lecktor* during my stay in Slovakia who had such an amazing deal. Susan was a marvelous cook, and I do not recall ever having the same dish twice. She introduced me to a custom that all cultures should adopt—Sugar Day. Sugar Day is the happiest day of the month. For the main meal, everything she would cook would be sweet. It wasn't unhealthy though. She prepared dishes like crepes with apricot jam, or some other fruit. Sometimes it might be a pastry made with poppy seeds. It was always excellent, and new to my palate. Each time we would eat together Susan sized me up, and seemed to be thinking to herself, *At least I have given him one more day of life.*

I needed to develop a strategy for teaching Samuel. We began by simply walking around the apartment. I would point to items, he would tell me the Slovak word, and I would teach him the English equivalent. After that, I began teaching him some basic verbs. I needed help from Susan with that. She spoke very little English, but she did speak German, so we were able to fall back on our second languages to get communicate. Toward the end of my stay, I was writing fairy tales with Samuel as the main character and having him read them to me. I don't know if I was the best English teacher Samuel could have ever had, but I know

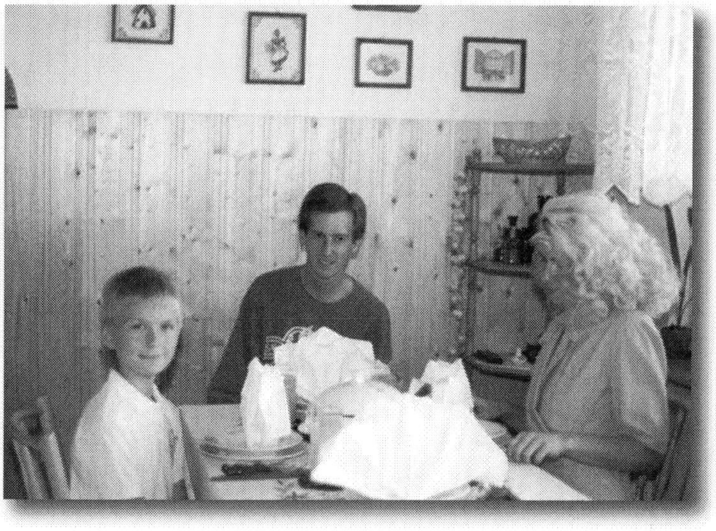

Lunch before a lesson with Susan and Samuel

he learned more English than if we had never met, and I met a family who showed me great warmth and provided me with insight into what family life was like in Slovakia.

Magdalena was a student in one of my morning classes. She was the only thirty-something in a group of eighteen-year-olds. She also stood out because she had Multiple Sclerosis. Europe in general, but Eastern Europe specifically, is not a good place to have to cope with a physical disability. Magdalena walked with a crutch, and each step appeared to be painful. Her wish to learn English stemmed—I believe—more from a need for human contact than from any need to pick up another language. Within a week she asked me if I would teach her privately. I agreed, and we decided to meet at her house a couple of times per week. She lived just west of the old town square across from the park. Her house needed of some serious renovation, but at one point it must have been a grand place. It was two-stories, and looked as though it was probably about 100 years old. To this point, I had not met a Slovak who lived anywhere other than a suburb like Sasova, with its identical grey high-rise apartments.

If ever there was a sad story, it was Magdalena. She had a husband who emotionally abandoned her following her MS diagnosis. He bluntly told her he no longer was attracted to her, and he only made one appearance during the six months I was tutoring her, and that was via telephone. She had two children under the age of ten. Both were boys and thoroughly out of control, and she had no hope of being able to reign them in because of her condition.

Magdalena's English seemed permanently stuck at the intermediate level, and I think she just wanted someone to talk to for a couple of hours per week. Because she was older, she had interests that were wider than the other students. We often sat in her living room and talked about politics, society, and culture; whatever she wanted. Sometimes, when she couldn't produce the English word she needed, she would fall back on her German, and we could piece things together from there.

Part of visiting a place instead of living there is to be blissfully ignorant of its problems. I have always tended to feel far safer in European cities than in American ones. The truth is that—to some degree—crime is everywhere. One afternoon Magdalena told me a story about her sister, who had emigrated to Germany. She told me she was murdered.

"No, you mean she died," I said. I was trying to be the good teacher and thought she had used the wrong word.

Magdalena replied, "No, Chrees. Murder. Man come into her house, and, um, how you say, dragged her down to basement, and cut off *hlava*, um, head."

Oh, fuck. I looked at Magdalena in complete shock and, after taking a sip of coffee, said, "Yes, murder is the correct word."

8

What's in a Name?

MAGDALENA LIVED ON TAJOVSKEHO ULICA (*ulica* is street), just across from the park. The park's nomenclature issues were indicative of problems across the country as it emerged from a half-century of oppression. As a rule, Slovaks have a history of being dominated. Their only stint as an independent nation was a bit of a façade since it came during World War II. Thanks to Neville Chamberlain and the Munich Conference, the Czechs had been taken over by Germany. Slovakia became independent under a puppet leader for the Nazi regime, Jozef Tiso. They did revolt against the Nazis but were brutally put down in what came to be known as the Slovak National Uprising (SNP). There is a museum dedicated to that event in Banska Bystrica. The exterior of the building looks like the soup bowl that Leave It to Beaver got stuck in. After this, the Soviets moved in. Given this history, it becomes more understandable why the Slovaks wanted to form an independent country when they had the chance, even if it might not have been the best idea economically to separate from Czechoslovakia.

When the Soviets took over, they began changing the names of landmarks, particularly streets and public spaces. When I was living there in 1993, the Slovaks were in the beginning stages of changing all of the names back to what they were in the pre-Soviet era. One problem this created was that directions could be insane. People used a hodge-podge of old and new street names, and sometimes following your nose was the best option.

Magdalena's neighborhood park was beautiful, filled with trees, and multiple paths that converged at a gazebo. There were also clay tennis courts. I would frequently take walks there after Magdalena's lessons. Under communism, the park had been renamed Lenin Park. It shouldn't surprise anyone that of all the names that needed to be changed, that one was at the top of the list. For whatever reason though, they failed to give it another name. I was told that no one remembered what the old name was. My guess is there was a certain amount of bureaucratic inefficiency in play. Regardless, the name Lenin was dropped. To add insult to injury, there are no definite or indefinite articles in the Slavic languages, so it wasn't even "The Park." It was just Park. Ah well, who doesn't love going to Park.

9

The Gastro Centrum

One night per week all of the English speakers gathered at a pub named the Gastro Centrum. There were twenty native speakers total, which included EFD, the British Council, and the Peace Corps. Slovaks interested in improving their conversational skills would come too. The food was basic, usually fried cheese and beer. Lots of beer. It was here that I learned one of my first important Slovak language lessons. I had had all of the beer I wanted (this stuff doesn't come out in a dainty glass; everything is a half-liter). The waitress came by and asked me in Slovak if I wanted another beer, "*Este jeden pivo, prosim*?"

"Uh, no," I replied. And another beer appeared. This happened two more times, before Merrill, slightly knackered, but more amused, chose to intervene.

He said, "Chris, in Slovak, *no* means yes."

"What are you talking about?" I slurred.

"Yes is *ano* and no is *nye*. She thinks you are saying yes you want another beer."

There are worse ways to learn a lesson and I did have time to sober up. The last bus left at 10:00 p.m. We walked the five miles from the city center to Sasova that night.

We met many of the people that would form our social network at the Gastro Centrum. There were David and Marie, who taught in two different schools in Banska Bystrica. It turned out they had an apartment up the street from us in Sasova. There was also Renata, who was particularly gifted at English. She had already spent considerable time in the United States and was interested in all things American. She had a sharp wit and was always actively engaged in whatever conversations were taking place. Merrill was particularly drawn to Renata, and they went from friendship to dating to engagement and marriage. I was home teaching in the United States when they got married, and was unable to attend the wedding, on May Day. I did call him the night before though.

"Are you sure you want to go through with it?" I jokingly asked.

"I have to," he replied. "I already slit the calf's throat."

Ah, Slovakia.

10

"Such a Typical Jew"

THE SLOVAKS I MET SEEMED to be in a certain degree of denial about their relations with Jews—both past and present. Tiso collaborated with the Nazis and sent a large percentage of Slovakia's Jewish population to death camps such as Auschwitz, which was only a few hours north of Banska Bystrica. The Slovaks I met rationalized his actions to me by pointing out that he had no choice, and that if he had not given the Nazis what they wanted, far more people would have died. In the minds of many Slovaks, it all just sort of worked out, and Tiso could be remembered as a noble figure who preserved their country. Unfortunately, in doing so, some Jews and Gypsies had to be sent to their deaths.

There was a middle-aged man in one of the classes that I occasionally guest-lectured who I had not particularly thought about it, but in hindsight, I should have realized he was Jewish. Although the United States has no shortage of problems in terms of prejudice, we are a nation of so many different groups, I don't think we always automatically think of what someone's potential religion is the first time we meet them. He had apparently been taking classes for years at the school and was never able to advance past the intermediate level. I knew him passingly well. When I encountered him, he was always eager to talk and try to engage me with his broken—yet far better than my Slovak—English.

Midway through the year, I was talking to a group of teachers and one of them brought up how much she despised this student. I was surprised.

"Why don't you like him?" I asked. "He tries so hard. He is always on time. He is eager to speak in class, even though it is obviously hard for him. What don't you like about him?"

"He is typical Jew," the woman replied.

"What do you mean?" I asked.

"You have listened to his English. It is terrible. He has been taking courses for years, and he doesn't get any better. But he won't stop. He just keeps trying, even though he will never be any good at it."

I was so shocked. She hated him for working hard, and all he wanted to do was better himself and learn a foreign language. In what I hope was the only moment that I insulted one of my hosts, I looked at the woman and said, "I understand why a Slovak would be unable to appreciate that sort of work ethic."

11

Hippy Dippy and Don't Like Gypsies

I am lumping the two negative stories about Slovakia together, because I think they belong together, and I would like to get any limited negativity that is in this book out of the way. Prejudice is a significant problem in Slovakia, and in Eastern Europe in general. Jews across all of Europe have faced violent attacks in recent years. All the people I met in Slovakia were incredibly gracious hosts. If it had ever occurred to them that they were offending me by making derogatory comments about other groups, they never would have done so. The fact that they spoke so freely, in my opinion, demonstrated how ingrained their prejudices were. They never considered anyone would ever think another way, much less be offended by their comments. This to me demonstrates how insidious prejudice and discrimination can become within a culture.

A student in my other morning class had interested me for some time. Her English was excellent. She dressed like a 1960's flower child. She was fascinated with the Beatles, and all things related to that era. She even had a peace symbol—sort of—that she wore as a medallion. It was actually a replica of a Mercedes symbol, but she was trying.

At about this time there had been a grisly murder of a Roma in the Czech Republic that had gotten widespread attention. She asked me if I knew about the incident. I did.

"Is good thing, no?" she asked.

"How could such a thing be good?" I asked.

"Gypsies are problem in our country. It is important that sometimes we show them who is boss."

I tried to steer the conversation back to the ideals that Miss Flower Power seemed to be fascinated with, but to no avail. When it came to the gypsies, those beliefs did not apply. The Roma issue remains in Slovakia and shows no signs of improving. The Roma population is inward looking and based on what I saw has a minimal interest at best in becoming a mainstream part of Slovak society. The Slovaks look down on the gypsies as inferior and have largely relegated them into an inferior caste. The tightness of the Roma community force them to the fringes of their Slovak communities. Ideally, if gypsies could develop a desire to enter mainstream Slovak society, and Slovaks would open their hearts to the gypsies, relationships could improve. Neither of these concepts appears likely to take root anytime soon.

12

I Have No Sense of Fantasy

THERE ARE A COUPLE OF major challenges to teaching in a post-Communist nation if you are an American. The first is that we don't realize how different it is to be raised in a democracy as opposed to an authoritarian regime. Free thought was not encouraged. Plus, in a Communist system, everyone theoretically is working together for the greater good. This belief system poses a challenge for a teacher who wants his students to think independently. Students in Slovakia were used to working in pairs. When I gave them an assignment that was to be done alone, they simply ignored the directions and worked together. I tried to introduce the concept of cheating to them, but the persistent reply was they were not cheating. They were helping each other.

One way I discovered to contain the cheating was to give writing assignments and tell them they were not allowed to work together. At first, they balked when I tried to give them creative topics. "Chrees, we have no sense of fantasy," many of them would exclaim. Finally, I decided to try something more concrete, and asked them to write about someone whom they admired that they would like to meet. The person could be living or dead. Interestingly, several of them chose to write about Audrey Hepburn, who had recently died. They were not interested in her movies, which had been made mostly before any of the students were born. It was her work with UNICEF that interested them and elicited their admiration. Although I knew about Hepburn's work in that arena, it never had occurred to me that other cultures might primarily view her through the lens of her humanitarian efforts.

13

Slovak Food

AT LEAST IN TERMS OF the Americans I met who were teaching in Slovakia, Southerners were in the minority. There was constant talk among the Americans about how horrible the food was in Slovakia. They were particularly bothered by the scarcity and lack of diversity of vegetables. They also did not like that frequently the only way restaurants seemed to prepare meat was by frying it. These were some salad loving people. I had always leaned too much toward meat and potatoes when it came to my culinary yearnings. Plus, frying is not likely to offend anyone from the great state of Alabama.

"How do these people live past forty?" a person asked during one of our weekly gatherings at the Gastro Centrum.

"I don't know," said another. "Everything they eat is fried meat or fried cheese. And the only things they eat with that stuff are potatoes."

"I know," I replied. "Isn't it great?"

Just for clarity, the Slovaks did have vegetables. However, they tended to only have what was in season and readily available in their stores. Under communism, trade was generally allowed only with like-minded nations. If you stop and think about it, almost all of the former Warsaw Pact nations were in cold climates, which is going to lead a lot of root vegetables. The Slovaks historically were a rural and farming people. The word "city" does not exist in Slovak. There are only towns (*mesto*). There are a few big towns, such as Bratislava, Kosice, and Banska Bystrica, but mostly there are villages. The diet we were living on in Slovakia was very much in line with the history and culture of our new settings. Rural farmers rarely come in from the fields hoping their wives have prepared them a good salad.

One word a traveler quickly learns when he goes into a Slovak restaurant is *vyprazanie* (fried). Besides the fried cheese (*vyprazanie syr*), which to me was a wonderful concept, there were also fried mushrooms (*vyprazanie sampiony*). Both of these were frequently considered an entrée on a pub menu. And they always came with the optional, but strongly encouraged *tartarsku* sauce, which is apparently Slovakia's primary contribution to world culture in the minds of many of its citizens.

"Chrees, do you know about *tartarsku,* er tartar sauce?" a colleague asked me while we were waiting on an order of fried mushrooms and drinking a beer.

"I believe I do," I replied.

"It was invented in the Slovakia," the person replied. "The only real tartar sauce is here."

To this day, I don't completely understand the tartar sauce phenomenon. Really, no matter how you try to explain it, everybody was a little too orgasmic over what was, in my opinion, a rather run of the mill condiment. However, it is again good to take a step back and look at the Slovak mindset. Historically, they had been peasant farmers. A variety of other nations had dominated them over the course of their history. The Slovaks were a good people who had been dealt a lot of bad hands of cards over the past 1,000 years. They did have, though, their tartar sauce. Within this context, the best thing to do is dunk that mushroom in the tartar sauce and chase it with a healthy swig of Slovak beer. There are far worse fates to have to endure.

I was not living entirely on Slovak Crowns; I also brought about 500USD. It is amazing how far that small amount of money went in 1993 Slovakia. As a result, I frequently ate at restaurants, rather than cook at home. Besides, there are only so many things you can make in a stock pot. There were several restaurant options even in 1993 in Banska Bystrica. After my morning classes, I would usually walk to the historic town square and find a place to eat that was always good with shockingly reasonable prices by Western standards.

The name Banska refers to mining. Banska Bystrica was a copper mining town that was controlled by the Fugger family of Germany during the 1300s. As a result of the success of their mining ventures, Banska Bystrica became a bit of a boom town and a large square was established with buildings designed with gothic architecture that were often quite ornate. By the time I arrived, many of the buildings were not in terrific shape, but the facades were well maintained. If you didn't look too closely, everything looked to be in remarkably good repair, and it was easy to imagine what it might have been like to live there during the latter part of the Middle Ages.

Along the way to the square was the Pizzeria Alba, which was a frequent stop for both Merrill and me. Pizza in Slovakia was different from anywhere else I have ever been. Tomato sauce does not exist. No one (and this became something that almost every American seemed to investigate at one point or another)

Looking down on Banska Bystrica

even understood what it was. I went to the store that sold Western products, and the only response I got to my queries were confused looks. Instead of tomato sauce, customers could order (for three crowns extra) a small serving of ketchup. I never was able to come to terms with ketchup on a pizza, but this dry version of a pizza did not particularly bother me, and with time I came to like it. Toppings were quite varied, although I tended to prefer the *slanina* (ham) pizza. One of the odder options was the pizza with *ovum.* It came with a big sunny side up egg in the center of it.

Tschibo, one of my favorite coffee brands, had opened a café on the main square in Banska Bystrica, and in the process remodeled one of the many 14th century buildings. In addition to a great cup of coffee, there were several cases of pastries. A morning pastry with a café au lait would set me back a whopping equivalent of fifty cents. Particularly during the cold months, Tschibo would frequently be a twice-a-day visit.

For street food, nothing could beat a *langos*. There was a stand near one of the roads that shot off from the square. *Langos* is really nothing more than deep fried dough. There were also a variety of toppings you could choose to add to it. Now that I am in my fifties, and know that I have the thrill of an EKG annually, it seems like a strange thing to eat, but few foods taste better than fried dough, and in a nation of heavy drinkers, it certainly went well with large quantities of beer.

On the other side of the square from Tschibo, Samuel renovated a building and opened a restaurant he named Fontana, for the square's fountain, that could be seen prominently from the restaurant's windows. He managed to raise a lot of capital

Banska Bystrica clock tower

for the remodel work, and also bought Italian china and flatware. My guess is that there had never been such a nice restaurant in town before. The menu was extensive as well. I was never clear what his business model was. Austrian tourists would frequently visit in tour buses, so he may have been hoping the drivers would steer their clients toward Fontana. Merrill's consistent comment was that he would like to be in a position to buy him out when he failed. My understanding was that over a quarter of a million dollars had been invested in renovating the building, which dated from the mid-1300s. Meals though, had to be priced so that locals could afford them, or no one would ever come and patronize the business. Ultimately, a three course meal cost about the equivalent of 5USD, which to the Slovaks at the time was remarkably expensive. That may seem silly, but remembering their salaries were set at about 100USD per month, consider how many people anywhere in the world would spend 5% of their income on one meal? The restaurant closed several months after it opened.

Some beliefs from the Middle Ages were held over into modern day Slovak food and drink culture. There was a pervasive belief that cold liquids were unhealthy and could make you sick. A guest came over to our apartment in February. Perhaps the only American thing that we tried to always have in our apartment was a bottle of Coca Cola, which we kept cold on our balcony. I asked the guest if she would like some and she said yes, only to recoil in mild horror when I pulled it off of the snow-covered balcony.

"Chrees, you are very brave boy," she said.

Absolutely and thoroughly lost, I inquired as to why.

"Drinking cold drinks make you sick."

This leads us to the exception to the cold rule. *Zmrzlina* (ice

Banska Bystrica Cathedral and Musuem

cream) is a Slovak obsession. It can be ten degrees below zero (and it sometimes was), and they would be walking around the square with an ice cream cone. No one was ever able to explain why a sip of a cold Coke (American champagne as it was referred to by someone I met in Rome once) would kill a person on the spot, but somehow the human body could withstand this sometimes two hits a day of ice-cold dairy.

14

Slovak Drinking

A FEW YEARS AGO, I was criticized by an acquaintance for "drinking like a European." That may be true, but having spent considerable time in Slovakia, to me that would be the height of moderation. Drinking like an Eastern European is taking alcohol intake to a completely different level. Slovaks seemed to think that anytime was the right time to drink alcohol. In my first week on the job, I was invited to go have a beer with Maros, who was one of my co-teachers.

"Chrees," he said, "I will teach you handball, Slovak national sport." He then made several drinking motions with his hand as though he was lifting a pint—pint, hell—half liter of beer.

There was a belief, which likely still exists, that a person was not drinking alcohol if they were drinking beer or wine. I actually had several people during my time in Slovakia tell me they did not drink alcohol. Then, later when I would see them at a bar drinking, they would explain that beer and wine didn't count. Perhaps beer and wine shouldn't have counted when compared to the other intoxicants that were in play. First, the concept of a mixed drink did not exist. Everything was a straight shot. Vodka was obviously popular, as was cognac, which I never quite understood. First, it seemed out of place, but second, I had never thought of it as a shooter. Regardless, a few shots and a person would be robbed of his inhibitions.

The other two drinks that were popular were an herbal liquor—that Slovaks also claimed could cure the common cold—called Becherovka. For clarification purposes, Becherovka will make you not care that you have the common cold, but I didn't get the impression that it had any curative properties. Think of it as more of a palliative. Zwack is a Hungarian herbal liquor that seemed to always turn up a lot. We liked it just for its name. Whenever we would score a bottle, David's refrain would be "We're getting Zwacked tonight!" There was also a hideous plum brandy named Slivovitz. Variations on Slivovitz could be found in each of the Eastern European countries. I really couldn't stand this one. To me, drinking it produced the sensation of swallowing pine needles.

A problem for Merrill and me, as well as the rest of the Americans I would imagine, is that we were novelties. The iron curtain may have been a metaphor, but there was virtually no contact between ordinary Slovaks and Westerners from 1948-1989, much less people from what the Soviet Union portrayed as the most evil place on earth, the United States. It seemed like everyone in every bar we went to wanted to buy us a drink. We were young and loved the free booze. We just couldn't handle the pace. One night we were out, and the shots kept coming. There was a plant in the window behind our table. Each time the drinks would come, everyone in the bar would shout "*na zdrovie*!" which means "to your health." We raised our glasses and when no one was looking dumped their contents into the plant. It may have been one of the most egregious acts of herbicide ever in the history of botany.

The bar we only went into in moments of desperation, or morbid curiosity, was the Cerveny Rak, or Red Lobster. It was a place where only the drunkest of drunks hung out. Men would be so completely wasted that they would piss their pants while standing at the bar and just keep on drinking, which led to a unique aroma. To make it more fun, the place served food. It was here that I learned what one person told me was an old Slovak expression: "Pissing in your pants will only keep you warm for so long." That is one of the universe's ultimate truths. In an effort to not slander institutions that still exist, and have potentially improved over time, the Cerveny Rak is still around, and based on pictures I found via Google seems to have made quite a few changes for the better. I was in Banska Bystrica in 2007, but did not stop by since it was never one of my hangouts.

This non-stop habit of drinking impacted the Slovaks both culturally and in terms of health. The men tended to drink a lot more than the women, and it was the women who got stuck cleaning up the men's messes, which meant dealing with the aftermath of their drunk husband's activities, and also taking care of the home and child. I met quite a few young people who didn't drink at all, and for them that included beer and wine. In conversations with them, they often explained that their parents, or grandparents, drinking habits led them to their belief that complete abstinence from alcohol was the best solution to have a chance at a healthy and happy life.

Although drinking to the point of being staggering drunk every night might be fun, it has no health benefits. The average age of death in Slovakia when I was there was seventy-three, and today has increased to seventy-seven. However, the men died an average of seven years before then women. These numbers were far worse than in the West, and could certainly be attributed in part to the nation's drinking culture. Maros and I were in his village's bar one Saturday and an old guy staggered in. He was disheveled, bald, and largely toothless. He was effectively the village drunk, which would have to have been a competitive title. Maros asked me how old I thought the guy was, and I guessed mid-seventies. The answer was forty-eight.

That night, Merrill joined us, and we attended a big party at Maros's family's house. They had a homemade wine that they were remarkably proud of. Just out of morbid curiosity, I would still like to find out what the alcohol content of the stuff was. There was also, of course, vodka, Slivovitz, Becherovka, and a host of other types of booze. I know Merrill was drunk, not because he was acting particularly oddly, but because I was seeing double, and his tolerance was not much different than mine. I

At the party in Maros's village

figured if I was in that bad a condition, he had to at least be drunk. We realized we had missed the last train back to Banska Bystrica. I think Maros wanted us to stay the night, and intentionally failed to alert us to the time.

I looked at Merrill and said, "We may die here."

We assured Maros that we knew there was another train and left without much of a plan. We ended up walking along the train tracks all the way back to Banska Bystrica, which was about seven miles, and from there onward to our place in Sasova. Between the bitter cold and the long walk, we were remarkably sober by the time we got home.

15

Weekend Getaway to Stara Lubovna

After about three weeks in Slovakia two EFD lecturers—Jan and Andy—arranged for a group weekend in Stara Lubovna, which is a ski town at the base of the High Tatras mountain range. As an Alabamian, I had no experience skiing (something that is still true today). I was, however, curious to see another part of the country.

The trip from Banska Bystrica to Stara Lubovna was difficult. Travel in 1993 Slovakia was ultimately efficient, yet certainly not luxurious. The bus ride lasted three hours, but there were no available seats. Merrill and I had to stand for all but the last half hour of the trip hanging onto a strap that extended from the bus's ceiling for dear life. Meanwhile, we became increasingly nauseous as the bus careened around icy curves. We were at the very front of the bus and spent the entire drive wondering if we were about to be thrown through the windshield. Not far from either of our thoughts was the aftermath of the bus crash we had witnessed on our initial journey to Banska Bystrica with Pan Biel.

That night we went to the Ducla Disco Club, which was another Slovak throwback to the 1970s. Teenagers always seemed to be in places like this, which seemed odd to me, since in the United States they wouldn't have been able to get inside what was effectively a glorified bar with a disco ball hanging from the ceiling. However, the rules about the drinking age in Slovakia, particularly then, always seemed to be quite vague. And, of course, we can go back to the concept that beer and wine were not considered alcohol by a lot of people in that culture.

The mayor showed up at Ducla that night. It turned out that there were twenty Americans in town, and that set a record for the most Americans ever in Stara Lubovna. I am not sure who was responsible for keeping up with such unusual statistics, be we accepted the information at face value. Before the night was over, a somewhat inebriated Merrill bought everyone in the bar a round of drinks. Since I knew he was not overflowing with money at the time I was somewhat shocked when I asked how he could afford to do such a thing, but did appreciate his answer of "When would I ever be able to afford to do something like this again?" Beer cost roughly the equivalent of thirty-three cents, and liquor didn't cost much more. We left the bar around 2:00 a.m. and walked a mile or so to Andy's place, who lived on the outskirts of the town. Andy's apartment made me realize the disparity of all of the lecturers' various living conditions and definitely made me appreciate my situation in Banska Bystrica. He had a room with two tiny beds and a table. He shared a nasty bathroom with a toilet that looked like it had new and previously undiscovered life forms growing in it. Until this point, Merrill and I had believed that we were living a minimalist lifestyle.

Saturday morning, we met at Iveta's, who was a Slovak—and part Roma—friend of Jan and Andy's. By the time we got to her apartment the entire group of EFD lecturers had arrived, and we were all scattered throughout her place. Much to my delight I could smell food cooking. On the table was a huge serving platter that was piled high with French toast. The platter was steadily being replenished with food by Iveta, who referred to the French toast as "an old family recipe." Slovaks are similar to most other Europeans when it comes to breakfast. It is generally "continental" and very light. I had not had what I considered a real breakfast in almost a month, and ate eleven slices. Iveta, to me, is one of the greatest exemplars of Slovak hospitality. She couldn't have been more than casual acquaintances with Jan and Andy, and she certainly did not know any of the rest of us. Still, she was willing to invite all of us into her home, and stand over a stove and cook for us until we could eat no more. I was able to talk to her some about her background. The Roma and Slovak populations rarely intermingle, but her parents met, fell in love, and were married. As an adult, she had chosen to move into—which I assume meant remain—mainstream Slovak society, rather than the more reclusive Roma one.

After thanking Iveta many times, we left to go skiing. Slovakia was having more of an icy winter than a snowy one. I was accustomed to neither, but knew these were not ideal skiing conditions. We took a bus to the small town of Vysne Ruzbachy and had to walk about three miles—while carrying skis and other supplies—from there to the ski lifts. Merrill and I were at a disadvantage, because we had already walked about two miles back and forth to Andy's apartment. By the time we arrived, I had developed a blister on my foot, and was exhausted from carrying ski equipment. The ski lifts were bizarre to me.

First, just to get to them, you had to try to walk on ice for a few hundred yards. Sliding hither and thither, I finally got to the lift, which was more like an individual schoolyard swing. Users were supposed to turn with their back to the rapidly approaching chair and get into what in tennis would be called the ready position. I tried this three times, and each time the lift would slide up, hit me solidly in the balls, and then swerve around me and move on. With my groin feeling like an abused punching bag, I told everyone they could slide down the mountain of ice without me, and left the group to find the ski lodge and beer.

As we were preparing to leave, a teacher from Poland who had brought a group of elementary school children to ski offered to drive all of us back to Stara Lubovna on their bus. It was one more example of the kindness of strangers in this part of the world, as well as at this time in history. It was also an opportunity for the children to practice their English with a group of Americans. They talked with all of us throughout the drive back.

Overnight, it snowed about five inches. We started the morning once again at Iveta's. She had spent the previous couple of hours peeling potatoes, and was now making French Fries for everyone, because she was out of eggs. We thanked her profusely, and then left to see the local castle before heading back to our separate Slovak worlds.

16

Banska Bella

All of the EFD lecturers, especially the guys, were warned about the opposite sex being particularly drawn to us. For purely economic reasons, we were a potential temptation. Just the fact that we were American made people naturally interested in us. For me it was Bella. She was a student for only one day in my class, because she was unable to pay the tuition. She was a frequenter of the Gastro Centrum though, and her English was quite good. I certainly noticed her, because she was attractive and quite a flirt, but had not thought of her much beyond that point.

Toward the end of February, Merrill and I decided to throw a party on a Thursday night. About thirty people came. Remembering Iveta's idea, we bought twenty pounds of potatoes. Everyone took turns at the stove with our only piece of cooking equipment, the stock pot, and made French Fries, while everyone else drank to their heart's content. The police visited the apartment twice, in an effort to try and get us to be quieter. The first time they came, they both looked like they had seen a ghost. Remember the Slovak custom of removing your shoes before entering an apartment. When we answered the door to our little apartment, the first thing the police saw was a pile of thirty pairs of shoes!

When we were still in the United States one of the popular TV programs was ABC's *Perfect Strangers*. Balki Bartokomus's accent as the immigrant from the island nation of Mepos was far too similar to the accent of some of the Slovaks. Slovaks often use nicknames, or diminutives when referring to people. Typically, the name is shortened and the letters "ko" are added at the end for males. We realized that Merrill would have been Merko, and I would have been Crisko. It didn't take long to decide that we should change that to the more traditional Crisco, and from that point on, I was often referred to as "The Crisco Kid." At one point during the evening Merrill and I reenacted Balki's "Dance of Joy."

I walked into the kitchen and shouted, "Merko!"

With equal gusto, he shouted "Crisco! Eet ees so good to see you, now we do the dance of joy!" We did the entire routine, with me jumping up and him catching me—sort of—at the performance's end. I am sure our downstairs neighbors were not thrilled having us as neighbors.

Much to my surprise, because she had not been invited (although everyone in the Greater Banska Bystrica Metropolitan Area was welcome), Bella showed up. We got to talking, and it was fun to have a conversation with someone who was reasonably fluent. We were more or less joined at the hip for the rest of the evening. At some point, I used the word "tempt" while talking, and she said she did not know the meaning of the word. Instead of trying to explain, I tossed her a small English-Slovak dictionary that was on the table. The first translation of tempt was seduce!

Before I knew what had happened, she had pounced on my 120-pound Alabama body, her lips locked against mine.

Ultimately, nothing came of my brief misadventure with Bella. We walked hand-in-hand to the bus stop at the end of the evening, and she made her way back home. I did see her on the square one evening several weeks later walking a gigantic dog. She said, "I'm taking my bitch for a walk." I've always wondered if she understood how funny that comment was, or if it was similar to confusing tempt and seduce.

17

A Trip to Prague

EVEN DURING THE EASTERN EUROPEAN winter we traveled when we could. It seemed important to make the most of our time in this part of the world. In late February, Merrill, Melanie (a *lecktor* from Florence, Alabama, living in the Slovak town of Martin), and I took the overnight train to Prague. Before leaving though, we had to go to a Name Day party for my colleague Maros.

Name days were a new concept to me. Effectively, just as everyone has a birthday, everyone has a name day. Name days were more aggressively celebrated than birthdays, with all of a person's friends bringing alcohol to their office, which naturally had to be opened on the spot and consumed. Maros had a lot of friends and loved to drink. He explained that we had to stop by for just a little while. I have a lifetime rule against mixing alcohol, and I developed it because of parties like this one in Slovakia. The good Lord (*Boh*), did not mean for us to mix different types of booze. We know that because of the hangovers doing so produces.

We staggered out of the former Communist Party Headquarters feeling worse than when we left Maros's village that night. It was barely noon, and we were plastered. The good news was we were packed and ready to go. We walked into the apartment, and Merrill promptly passed out. I set the alarm on my trusty Seiko watch before doing the same. I woke up to the alarm at 5:00 p.m., and shook Merrill awake. We took turns throwing up, and then headed to Pizzeria Alba for dinner.

"What are you going to have?" Merrill slurred.

"The ham," I replied.

"I want something different. I'm going to try this Pizza Ovum."

Thirty minutes later this pizza is plopped in front of Merrill. Looking half crestfallen and half confused, and obviously forgetting that ovum means egg in Latin, he said, "Someone cracked an egg on my pizza." Then he ate the whole thing. An hour later we were on the train to Prague.

Prague in February is absolutely frigid, so we spent a lot of time ducking into cafes, as well as bars, to warm up. The endless series of Gothic style buildings covered in snow is incredibly striking though. Merrill had never seen the city, and had not understood why I was so smitten with it. The realization hit him instantly. After he had a few minutes to think about it, he said, "It's like being in the middle of a really big Batman movie!" To this day, I continue to value my friendship with Merrill because of his keen analytical insight.

When we arrived at the train station, a man approached us and offered us an apartment in the center part of the city for $20 per night. I probably, wouldn't recommend anyone get in a stranger's car after meeting for the first time in a setting like a train station. However, he was not particularly imposing, and there were two of us. Plus, we were young and thought we were more or less indestructible. The man turned out to be perfectly

Castle Hill in Prague

legitimate, and took us to the apartment, which was everything he had promised. The heat, which was coal powered was only to be used when we were there. He showed us how to light the pilot. It was an entire apartment that was fully furnished in a major European city, and it was ours for twenty bucks. This was something we could definitely get used to.

We left the apartment and I led us to the cellar restaurant I had found on my last trip that was on Wenceslas Square. I had begun to feel a tad sorry for waiters, because as soon as they would see Americans coming in, they would get this glow about them, because they would think it was going to be a major payday. There was nothing about Merrill and me when we were travelling back then that screamed rich American. I think everyone just equated American with rich. Both of us ordered the goulash soup with dumplings. The taste was good, and it was a hearty meal that prepared you for the cold outside. As always, it went so well with beer. The poor waiter looked crestfallen.

Prague had changed so much since my previous visit in 1991. The Americans had landed, and were trying to recreate Hemingway's 1920s experiences in a new locale. By 1993 there were 50,000 American ex-pats living in Prague. Whereas not quite two years earlier, I could rarely find a native English speaker, now the long-haired, pierced, goatee-sporting American was ubiquitous.

To me, one of the more interesting aspects of touring Prague was the prevalence of Dixieland jazz bands. Leaving Wenceslas Square, we took the short walk to the Old Town Square, and as soon as we entered, there was a quartet that was exactly where I had seen them on my previous two visits, playing for tips. I later found out that playing jazz was viewed as a form of rebellion against the Communist regime, because it was such a non-structured, non-conformist type of music.

Dixieland Jazz band in Prague's Old Town Square

Prague Old Town Square

In addition to all of the American people, American consumerism had arrived in Prague. There were already two McDonalds and one Kmart. Kmart, in one of their less-slick moves, would go on to buy all of the state-run department stores in what was Czechoslovakia. The name of the chain they purchased was Prior. Kmart never caught on in that part of the world. Slovaks, in particular, were not a rich people. As a result, when they shopped, they wanted a good price, and merchandise that would last. In their opinion, Kmart offered neither. In a moment of desperation, Kmart in Banska Bystrica started running a bus that drove around the town and would pick up anyone who was willing to be taken for free to their store. They ultimately sold out to Tesco. No one seemed to be eager to hop on the Kmart bus.

Before one of the original Priors was taken over by Kmart, I bought a black overcoat (*kabat*) at the one in Banska Bystrica. The coat I had brought with me was remarkably inadequate for the Eastern European winter that we were in the middle of enduring. I still have it today, and although it may not be the most stylish articles of clothing in my wardrobe, it will definitely keep the wearer warm.

Our friend Melanie had traveled to Prague separately with Cary, another EFD lecturer who was living in Dolny Kubin, Slovakia, and that night we went with them to a Reggae bar. They had met and taken the train together. There was an obviously American guy who stayed on the dance floor all night. He was skinny and tall, had long red hair and a red beard, and a bright green shirt on.

I looked at Merrill and said, "Jesus, he looks like Jesus."

We spent the rest of the evening trying to get Melanie to dance with Green Jesus, who never left the dance floor. He would move his feet back and forth in the same two-step moves, as he shook his hair back and forth, while holding a beer that he somehow never spilled.

Europeans in general never got the message about cigarettes causing cancer, and the reggae bar was oppressively smoky. I decided to leave my compatriots, who were having a good time, and cabbed it back to our apartment, taking the only key. I went inside, lit the pilot light on the heater, turned it up as high as it would go, and fell into my bed. About an hour later I awoke to

Merrill and Melanie pounding on the door, something they had apparently been doing for over twenty minutes while I was sleeping/passed out so hard, I hadn't heard. Merrill said it was like walking through the gates of Hell when I opened the door, and that the heat literally hit him in the face. It must have been over ninety degrees in that place. It was comfortable to me, I told him.

We had a few more days off, and in spite of the forecast which warned of significant snow, we decided to take a train to Wroclaw, Poland. It was described as a city of canals, and effectively the Venice of Poland. When we arrived, Wroclaw was in what I would call as a state of white out. There was little hope of playing Tommy Tourist in weather like that, and our only option was a tactical retreat to Banska Bystrica. Before we could do that, we needed to change currency into Zloty so we could buy train tickets. No one in the train station was willing to change our Crowns, and credit cards were a foreign concept, so we would need a bank. A guy gave us directions to the only bank that would change Czechoslovak Crowns. Trying to follow his directions as closely as possible, with me staying only a pace behind Merrill—any farther back and I couldn't see him—we set off in the storm. The bank turned out to be almost directly across the street from the train station! We never could figure out why the guy sent us on such a hike, or if something was just lost in translation, but we now had money and train tickets, and just had to try to find a warm place to wait.

We headed to the ticket booth in the train station and requested two tickets. Wroclaw, also known by the German name Breslau, had a large German-speaking population, so I was handling the transaction. The attendant kept asking something about times and movies. I was clueless and thought I was misunderstanding something with my not-so-perfect German skills. Merrill looked up and saw the word Kino above the attendant's counter. There was an actual movie theatre in the train station! We ended up watching a film called *The Lover*. There is nothing like watching a sexually charged film in a Polish train station. You will keep your eyes directly forward, for starters. I also couldn't help but think about the true victim in Pee Wee Herman's situation—the guy sitting in front of him. Ten hours later we were quite happy to be back in our apartment. The trip hadn't ended as we had hoped, but we did have an adventure and lived to tell the tale, so it wasn't all bad.

18

Slovaks and Capitalism

Although Slovaks were not as completely consumed with their jobs as Japanese and American workers are often labeled, they certainly worked hard at what they did. Plus, even with state price controls—which were gradually being diminished and would eventually go away—they were not able to have many of the luxuries that Americans had. The irony was that as long as they stayed in Slovakia, they could afford most of their needs and many of their wants. Their currency had so little value though, that they were unable to afford to go anywhere else. Prices could sometimes seem bizarre to Americans. I picked up a prescription one time when I had a cold, and the price was one Crown—the rough equivalent of three American cents.

Slovaks tended to believe that everyone in the United States was rich, and many dreamed of one day moving to America. I frequently tried to explain that while many Americans were rich, many more were extremely poor, in ways that Slovaks could never imagine. Most impressions they had of the United

States were from movies, and they had trouble imagining any version of America other than the land of riches that they knew from film. Sometimes at the Gastro Centrum we would talk about the need to take the Slovaks on a poverty tour of the United States, just so they could witness the imbalance between rich and poor.

A common lament that I often heard was, "Why am I not rich, I work hard?" There were no one-sentence answers to that question. The Slovaks were traditionally agrarian. There was also a tradition of coal mining in the eastern part of the country. The Communists had redistributed both land and wealth once they took over. They also—in the name of equality— diminished the salaries of professions that typically would have been viewed as high-end jobs in the United States, such as doctors and lawyers.

Slovaks had a minimal number of exportable products. They had one beer that was and is exported, *Zlaty Bazant* (Golden Pheasant). Their wine, while priced well wasn't of a quality that it could have been internationally competitive. Coal was something that until recently everyone has viewed as the fuel of the past. The main cash crop was apparently potatoes.

With inherited wealth not an option, price controls in place, and many salaries low for the education and expertise required for professional positions, it was hard to see how the Slovaks were going to develop a wealthy class in a legitimate fashion very quickly. A burgeoning mafia though, was starting to develop.

As I walked into work one day, a teacher stopped me and asked, "Chrees, did you hear about the murder last night?"

I hadn't.

"Man refused to pay mafia," she said. "They came back that night and shot him nine times with a 'Yuuzzy.'"

19

David and Marie

DAVID AND MARIE WOULD BECOME our two closest American friends in Banska Bystrica. They lived up the street from us on Ulica Tatranska and had a washing machine that was actually recognizable. The one in our apartment might hold a pair of jeans, which it somehow managed to shred during the washing process.

We had a weekly laundry night on Sundays starting around 5:00 p.m. While our clothes washed, we would all have dinner, and then move on to our weekly bit of English language entertainment, *The Simpsons* followed by *Star Trek: The Next Generation*. These were the only two English language television programs we were able to watch in Slovakia. Television would be followed with the Howard Stern radio show. David and Marie were both from New York, and they had friends who weekly sent audio tapes of the show. When I look back on it now, as repugnant a creature as Howard Stern is, only a country like the United States could have produced him, which did make him an appealing slice of home while we were visiting this frigid foreign land.

David and Marie were different from any couple I had met previously. I don't consider myself to be insulated to the degree that many Southerners can be, but I had never been around a young New York couple. They were clearly in love, but anything could become a low-grade fight; if not an outright fight, then certainly an intense negotiation. Marie could not have been more than about 5'2"—and had the personality of a somewhat benign Tasmanian Devil. David was at least 6'3", and very angular. He was more of a peacemaker than Marie, but knew how to stand his ground. He had a marvelously dark sense of humor. One evening around 1:00 a.m. we were making the long trek back to Sasova from a party in Banska Bystrica. The conversation had turned to Slovak attitudes toward the "Roma situation," and the all too common attitude the Slovaks had of "ain't no Roma like a dead Roma." Combined with their record with the Jewish population during World War II, it was fair to say that the Slovaks did have a few failings relating to ethnic minorities in their country. Walking in front of us on the dimly lit road, David stretched out his long arms toward the sky, inhaled deeply and loudly, and exclaimed, "It just isn't the same without the smell of burnt Jews and Gypsies in the air!"

Possibly, more than anyone else among the Americans teaching in Slovakia, David wanted to prove that the Slovaks were wrong in their attitudes toward the Roma population. He was right, but his method did not work so well. Headed for lunch one day he passed a Roma who was begging for money. He invited him to come with him to the restaurant, and they ate and had a couple of beers. Then, in order to complete his sociological experiment, he left the money to pay the tab on the table and excused himself to the restroom. When he returned, the Roma was gone and so was the money. The lesson, of course, was not that the Gypsies were inherently bad; rather, they were marginalized and poor. In that situation, people will seize what opportunities they can, and that includes taking advantage of well-intended people.

20

Communication

COMMUNICATION WAS ALWAYS A CHALLENGE, regardless whether with family back in the United States, or with friends and colleagues within Slovakia. Only 25% of Slovaks had telephones in their homes in 1993. Communication with people outside of the Eastern Bloc was discouraged if not outright prohibited by the Communists.

Everything we were doing to maintain contact with other people seems bizarre in our new era of instant communication. Telegrams were still a common way to get messages to people in Slovakia. We would frequently get telegrams in Banska Bystrica letting us know plans for a get-together somewhere else in the country. We would then show up, or not, and it was just understood there was no time to send a response, so there were no hard feelings.

Communicating with family back home was even more of a challenge. I carried an AT&T telephone credit card, which was supposed to make calling home easy. All I had to do was tell the operator the number, and my family took care of the bill. There was only one problem with this plan—Slovaks did not understand what credit cards were. They were an exclusively cash economy and did not have any idea how this piece of plastic I was holding up could have any value.

Generally speaking, international calls needed to be made from the post office. It seemed like everyone who worked in Banska Bystrica's post office was a very matronly *babushka* type. The first time that I went in and explained that I wanted to call the United States using my credit card, I was told that it was impossible. We argued for about fifteen minutes before I finally wrote down the AT&T operator's number and just told them to dial it. I then went into a booth where the babushka would direct the call. After that I could give an American operator the number and everything went smoothly. Eventually though, we realized we were occasionally being listened to by the postal workers. Once, while Merrill was talking to his mother, the operator broke in and accused him of essentially hijacking their phone system, since it was supposedly impossible to call the United States in the manner that we were doing.

The best way to call home if luck was on your side was using a pay phone. A local call was three Crowns. Obviously, if you had to feed the phone for every minute on an international call, you would quickly go broke. However, the whole telephone system was fairly primitive, and sometimes, if you put in your three Crowns like you were making a local call, you could call the United States and it would go through. After that, you could talk as long as you wanted. It never seemed to work twice in a row, and there didn't seem to be any rhyme or reason as to when you would discover one of these magic phones. After a night of drinking though, it was sometimes fun to walk around the square and see if I could call home for free. Sometimes I was a winner with this Slovak version of the lottery; sometimes I wasn't.

Sasova, Slovakia

The author with two of his students, Andrea and Martin

Slovak class

The author's Slovak bus pass

"Merrill, David, Marie and I visited the fairytale-like Bojnice castle on a day trip in March. There is a zoo next door to the castle."

"On the way to Piestany, we stopped to see Trencin Castle, which stands guard over the town with the same name. I snapped this picture before going up to tour the building. It was so good that we ended up making it the cover photo for the book."

21

Going to the Movies

WE FREQUENTLY WENT TO THE movie theatre in Banska Bystrica. I actually went to see far more films in Slovakia than I ever had in the United States. Most of the movies that were shown were recent American releases, and they were screened in English with Slovak subtitles, which worked out well for the native English speakers in attendance. I found that I also would pick up a little bit of Slovak vocabulary with each film, because I couldn't help but try to read the subtitles as the movie played. For instance, to this day, I know that *Zlato Oko* means Goldeneye. I have no idea how this informational nugget will ever be of benefit to me, but I am continuing to hold out hope.

The movie theatres, to me, were where a visitor could witness how oppressive Communist society had been. There were assigned seats (Communists liked order). The assigned seats did not particularly bother me, but what I couldn't figure out was why it really mattered so much in what was often a largely empty movie theatre. If you did not sit in the correct seat though, you would quickly find out that you had committed an offense against the house rules. As the recent television ad used to say, "There's an app for that," in the case of the movies in Slovakia, "There's a babushka for that." Theatre patrons were monitored by two babushkas throughout the course of the entire film. I never noticed one of them ever turning to watch any of the movies. They paid exclusive attention to the audience. If someone was in the wrong seat, they immediately moved in to correct the situation. If an audience member put his foot on the chair in front of him, watch out, because his world was about to come to an abrupt end.

The whole situation was bizarre. One of the things I dislike about going to the movies in the United States is how rude the audiences are. The Slovaks had solved the problem, but I didn't particularly enjoy Big Brother, or in this situation, Fat Grandmother, constantly spying on me and telling me what to do. If nothing else, a trip to the movies was a window, albeit a small one, as to what life was like under Communist rule.

22

Communism Explained with an Apple

I WAS HAVING A DRINK with Maja one afternoon in April. The previous day I had had a particularly frustrating American-living-in-another-country type of day. Struggles with different nations' systems and traditions is normal in any country, but in post-Communist Europe, it was sometimes particularly frustrating to an American. A lot of the systems the Communist leaders had developed were clearly meant to break the human spirit. Alcohol was priced so cheaply by the state that consumers were encouraged to buy beer and liquor rather than non-alcoholic options. A large percentage of the population were informants to the secret police, which kept people from feeling they had any freedom to speak their minds in public, and sometimes even within the confines of their own homes. And then there were the lines. There were lines for everything.

On this particular day, I had just wanted to run in a grocery store and buy a Coke. The line to get a basket was about ten people deep. Once I had the basket, I had to fight my way through the huddled masses in the tiny store in order to find my one item. I then had to wait for about twenty minutes for the surly clerk to take my money. I couldn't believe that I had just spent a half hour to purchase something I could have gotten out of a machine in the United States.

As we poured our second glass of wine, I looked at Maja and told her that I thought I finally understood what life must have been like under Communist rule. With that statement, I related the tragedy of the Coca Cola.

Maja's face darkened, and she said, "Let me tell you what life was like under communism. It is 6:00 a.m. and there is a knock at the door. It is your neighbor who tells you that there are bananas at the grocery store. You grab a bag, run to the store, where you stand in line for two hours, the entire time praying that you will be able to get one piece of fruit for each member of your family. That is what communism was like."

I apologized for my rudeness, which was unintended. I was just a twenty-two-year-old stranger in a strange land, trying to figure out how the country currently functioned, and how it had operated in the past. With that said, it was just plain arrogant for someone who comes from a land of endless privilege to think he can claim to truly empathize with someone who spent their entire life under a totalitarian regime.

Wine has soothing properties though, and Maja was fast to forgive my faux pas. She also related her personal history, and it helped me understand why I had hit such a nerve with my comment. When the Communists came to power her family had an apple farm that had been in the family for generations. Over a period of years, the Communists took section after section of the farm until it was gone. They did graciously let the family keep the house they had in Nitra.

As a result of the family losing the farm, Maja's grandfather, who had been an optician, became an outspoken critic of the Communist regime in Slovakia. For this, Maja would be punished. Her dream as a child was to become a lawyer. As she prepared to graduate from high school, she applied to go to the university in Bratislava. She was told that the government would not allow her to have such an important job as a lawyer. However, because the government was generous, they would allow her to attend college. She could only study to be a teacher, though.

To me, this story sums up how soul-sucking communism could be. The government set out (and succeeded) to crush a young girl's dreams. Then they forced her into a profession in which she had no interest. Maja was remarkably good at her job, and the students seemed to genuinely respond well to her. Every day though, she went to work at a job she never wanted to do. Maybe it was good that the alcohol was so cheap.

23

A Trip to the Doctor

EARLY IN MY STAY IN Slovakia, like all the other English teachers, I had to visit a clinic for a physical exam. I hadn't been looking forward to it. Others had been sharing their stories, and many of them did not leave me feeling optimistic about my visit. At the minimum, I didn't look forward to trying to discuss healthcare with someone who likely did not speak English.

Because nothing could be simple, I had to take a train from Banska Bystrica to Martin. Martin is actually much smaller, but the clinic I was ordered to go to was there. I arrived early and walked through the town briefly. Not finding much to see, and wanting shelter from the cold, I went into a bar and figured I could have a couple of beers and get warm until my appointment. The Slovaks really had way too much of an obsession with the 1970's United States. The bar had a very no-tell-motel lounge kind of a feel to the place. And, of course, there was the requisite disco ball. After a couple of beers, I was ready to go face the music.

I signed in at the clinic and awaited my turn. I walked back and was greeted by Dr. Babushka. In hindsight, perhaps it isn't a good idea for a nation's people to ingest so many carbohydrates. She did a brief exam, that involved a lot of miming, which I assume established that I was more or less healthy. Then she motioned for me to drop my pants. I acted like I didn't understand, but she repeated the gesture. I unbuckled my jeans and dropped them. Dr. B. sat down on a stool, and swiftly took my quickly retreating pecker in her hand, lifted it up, and turned it side to side. Then, she looked up and said "*Dobre*!" which means good. I had always thought so, but it was good to have my suspicions confirmed.

24

Learning to Count to Twenty-one in Piestany, or Red Means Dead

AMONG THE TEACHERS WHO I thought were almost as lucky in where they ended up working as Merrill and I were the crew who wound up teaching in Piestany. Piestany is a spa town, which led to it having a lot of tourists. It also had a lot of amenities that other towns did not have, which meant that in addition to all of this iron-rich (meaning rusty) water that the Slovaks believed had healing properties, there were more restaurants, better stocked stores, and more things to do in general, including gambling.

I truly don't have the disposition for gambling. I am nervous by nature, and even managed somehow to develop two stomach ulcers by the age of sixteen. With that said, wherever I go, I want to have, if not the full experience of the place, then at least I want to dip my toes in the water. Merrill had much more experience with gambling. He had been to Las Vegas several times while in college. His native Colorado has also taken some of the old mining towns that were largely abandoned and "casinofied" them, in an effort to keep them alive.

We knew several weeks in advance that we would be going to Piestany, and that casinos would be involved. Merrill had a battery powered blackjack game that I practiced on for about three weeks. I eventually became fairly good at it, but now it was time to put my abstract skills to the test for real. We walked into the casino—two wild and crazy guys from Banska Bystrica—and headed straight for the Blackjack table. I had already decided that I was willing to lose 100 Crowns and nothing more. We started playing, and I won the hand. And I won again, and again. I was up to 500 Crowns. The experience had an odd impact on me. I was trembling slightly, and I could feel sweat starting to creep down my sides. I lost the next hand, which dropped me down to 400 Crowns, and I decided to walk away with what I had already won. To put this all in perspective, remember the exchange rate was thirty Crowns to one dollar. I was ultimately panicking as I risked a total of three dollars at the casino. Put in the context of the local economy though, that 100 Crowns was a lot of money. Thinking in terms of beer, it was the equivalent of ten half-liter bottles. It was also potentially anywhere from three to five meals out at a restaurant, depending on how a customer ordered.

Merrill was willing to risk a larger amount of money. He started with 500 Crowns, and was not faring well. He won a couple of hands—but lost far more. When he was down to about fifty Crowns, he told the dealer he was done, and we walked away. We headed toward the exit. Before we had walked very far, he noticed a Blackjack table where no one was playing.

The dealer had it ready to go, and had the cards neatly arranged on the table. Merrill walked up to the table, looked at the dealer and said, "Shuffle." He won eight straight hands and walked out with 1,500 Crowns!

We spent the next day with Gloria and three of the other teachers. There were many restaurants to choose from, but they wanted to make lunch at their place. They were creating what every other American visiting Slovakia would have considered a delectable treat. The meal was nothing but salad, and they had visited every grocery store in the town so they could create this American-style vegetarian concoction. All I could think was, *I want some deep fried meat or cheese*. Possibly, I had stayed in this country far too long already. I knew there would have to be a pub not far in our future, so I sat there and tried to gnaw on a lettuce leaf and listen to the conversation.

By being older, Gloria had a frame of reference that the rest of us could not claim. As we talked about impressions of Slovakia, she told us that if we ever wondered what the United States was like in the 1940s, it was quite similar to what we were experiencing here. Particularly in terms of choices. There were far fewer brands, far fewer telephones, and far fewer medical services. It was as though the West had evolved after World War II, and Slovakia and the rest of the Eastern Bloc had been stunted because of the Soviet Union. She also helped us understand the impact of the Cold War, as well as real war on everyday people.

Gloria ran a travel resort in Minnesota on one of the lakes. In her sixties, she had decided she wanted to take some time for herself—and was letting a partner handle the business while she spent the year teaching in Slovakia. Tending to the business had fallen to her after her husband had returned from the Korean War, shell-shocked. He never recovered, and spent some time in therapy, but the army was less concerned about such problems in the 1950s. He was obsessed with the Communist threat—and tended to see the enemy at every turn. During one Christmas season they were hosting their two young grandchildren. Gloria put them to bed in matching red pajamas. She woke up during the night to realize her husband was not by her side. She immediately began looking for him and found him standing over the children's beds with a gun. The red pajamas had triggered his PTSD, and he thought the children were Communists. She was able to talk him down and take the gun. I don't think the children ever woke up or knew what had happened.

25

Sick in Slovakia

One of Maja's classes that I particularly enjoyed was an intermediate group of professional adults. One of the students in that class was a medical doctor who was the director of the Polyclinik in Banska Bystrica. His name was Dr. Moravic, and he was always eager to talk, and wanted to learn about my life in the United States, but also enjoyed sharing insights about life in Slovakia. He sometimes joined Maja and me for a drink after class, and we talked about a variety of subjects. The one that stuck with me was the very low bar to become a doctor in Slovakia. Effectively, in not much more time than it takes to get a master's degree in the United States, you could be a full-fledged doctor in Slovakia during the Communist era. Doctor Moravic had studied at Charles University in Prague, and from what I could gather was one of the best physicians in town.

In a climate as harsh as Slovakia is, it is no small wonder that Merrill and I both eventually got sick—which happened in March. I never knew what we had, but it was something between a severe cold and tuberculosis. It became clear on a

Friday morning that we were both very sick, and this was something that was not going to go away without professional assistance. I asked Maja to call Dr. Moravic's clinic for me and make an appointment. She said that he had mentioned to her in the last class that he was going to be out of town until Monday, so I asked her to make an appointment for that morning.

All of the Slovaks I knew—particularly the women—were remarkably nurturing toward me. Part of this as I have mentioned before was caused by my weight. They thought I wasn't eating, when in fact I was just skinny. I think they also didn't want to be blamed for killing the American who had been sent to help them.

The department head, Mira, came to me and said, "I know doctor. He can see you immediately."

I thanked her and said through a coughing fit that I could wait until Monday and see Dr. Moravic.

Mira persisted, "No, you are very sick boy. You should go to doctor now."

This went on for some time, and finally an exasperated Mira asked, "Why will you only see Dr. Moravic?"

Through my sore throat, I croaked, "Because he studied in Prague."

That ended the conversation, and I know my response had been impolitic. It was true and to the point though. The Slovaks and their medical beliefs were bizarre in some cases, and humorous in the abstract, but if I was the person who was sick, I wanted to go to someone that I knew was competent, and not someone who would send me off to a spa to drink rusty water then wait to see what would happen.

Slovaks often believed that spas could cure all of their illnesses. The government would allow them considerable time off if they were under a doctor's care to spend one or two months, and sometimes longer at spas, where they believed the water had curative powers. When visiting these places, Slovaks would take as many empty plastic soda bottles as they could carry. The bottles were orange with rust, filled at the springs, and then taken home to be consumed. I suppose I am cynical by nature. When I was a child, I went to Ponce de Leon State Park in Florida, where a park ranger told my family that according to legend, if we drank the water, we would stay young forever. When I look at my hairline in the mirror, I know that was a lie, because I drank an entire bottle of that stuff.

The reason for the medical profession's reliance on spas was not necessarily because the physicians or patients believed there were any curative properties in the waters at all, although certainly some of them thought there were. It was a delaying tactic caused by the Communists' reign. As a result of poor pay, people were not interested in learning how to do the difficult job of being a doctor. With a shortage of doctors, patients had to be treated on priority basis. However, if they had a condition that might be made worse by stress, they needed to be sent to a place where they would stay calm and relaxed. And this is how a system was created that would send patients who were in need of an angioplasty—a procedure that can almost be had on demand in the United States—to a spa for two or three months, until a surgeon could work them in.

In addition to believing that a cold Coca Cola would kill a person, Slovaks also believed that some other American sodas—obviously served at room temperature—could save a life. In a conversational exercise one of my students told me that Fanta Orange had cured her aunt's leukemia. I was convinced something must have been lost in translation even though her sentence was fairly straightforward.

"You're sure it was leukemia?" I asked.

"*Ano*, uh, yes," she replied.

I studied her closely, and said, "The only thing I know of that Fanta Orange cures is healthy teeth. Are you sure she didn't have chemotherapy treatments, or some other help from doctors."

The girl thought for a minute, and then said, "She had that too, but one day she drink entire one-liter bottle of Fanta Orange, and she was cured next day."

So now we know, I thought. I must now return to my land across the ocean and share this great discovery so that many lives can be saved.

Still sick, Merrill had now caught my malady as well. We felt horrible that weekend, and couldn't see Dr. Moravic until Monday, but did have one commitment. Merrill and Renata's relationship continued to become more serious, and he had promised that we would do a brief radio interview on a show she hosted that Saturday. She translated everything into Slovak during the interview, which was good, because I can't imagine how anyone could have understood us on the radio, since we could barely speak. First thing Monday morning we were at Dr. Moravic's office. After a quick exam he wrote a prescription, which cost one Crown—that is the equivalent of three cents—to fill. In a few days we were once again fit as the proverbial fiddle.

26

Nothing is More American than Mexican Food

AFTER WE HAD BEEN IN Slovakia for a couple of months several of us noticed that we were missing something that is a very basic creature comfort in the United States—Mexican food. All of us were fresh out of college, and one of the cuisines we could all count on during that period of our lives to be cheap and hearty could be found at one of the many Mexican restaurants that seem to always be exist in college towns. And, of course, there were the margaritas. We decided to have a Mexican night at our place.

Of the two of us, Merrill was the expert in terms of his knowledge of Mexican food. My belief in this fact was based on Denver's proximity to Mexico itself, and a large immigrant population that had moved from Mexico to Colorado. He figured out how to create a variation of *queso* with the cheese Slovaks use for frying, and also made refried beans. What we were really after was tequila. No one in Slovakia had apparently ever heard of it. We decided that each American would be responsible for bringing one bottle of tequila, and hoped that by tasking everyone, we would find enough for the party. Finding any kind of margarita mix was out of the question, so this would be a Slovak variation on Mexican night. Beer and shots would be the order of the evening.

I began asking students and teachers at work where I could source a bottle, but no one knew what tequila was. Then, I remembered the Western goods store that Josef had introduced me to. It took several minutes to explain to them what I wanted, but eventually they were able to produce their only bottle.

Among the things we learned the night of the party were, first, that no one in Slovakia had any concept of what tequila was. Second, we discovered that there were more liquor stores in Banska Bystrica than possibly in any major urban setting in the United States. Finally, we found out that several of these stores did have a bottle of tequila that they had acquired—most likely accidentally—and it had been gathering dust somewhere in the back of the shop for several years. I remain fully convinced that by the night of the event we had bought every bottle of tequila in the town. Everyone who came had a story of their tequila scavenging adventure, with Marie having my favorite.

When she arrived at liquor store number five on her quest, she approached the babushka behind the counter. When she inquired as to whether she had any tequila, the woman replied, "*Nye viem,*" meaning she didn't know what it was. Marie persisted though. She had been about to give up when she noticed on the very top shelf something that stood out in Slovakia. It was a large sombrero that was virtually covering a lone bottle. She pointed at it. The old woman looked at her, seeming to try to size up her adversary. Marie was a true New Yorker. She wasn't going to give up. She pointed again at the hat. The babushka had to go into the back of the store to retrieve a ladder. She climbed to the second to last step and reached for the bottle. Removing the sombrero, she then blew as hard as she could, and dust and other debris flew off the glass and drifted down in a dirty shower toward Marie below. She had herself a bottle of tequila. And a hat.

Sometimes, it seems amazing that all of us did not develop cirrhosis during our stay in Slovakia. I have no idea how many beers I had that night, and Marie and I both traded shots of tequila, which totaled seven a piece. She had arrived Davidless. He had to teach a class and then was going out with colleagues afterwards. Embracing my inner Southern gentleman, and also realizing her much less elongated frame had not absorbed the booze as well as mine had, I walked Marie up Tatranska to her apartment. I didn't pay much attention as we rode the elevator up. We stepped out into the hall and she inserted the key in the lock, which wouldn't turn.

"Fucking Slovakia!" she slurred. "Nothing here ever works."

She continued battling the lock for a couple of minutes, as I cast an inebriated gaze around the hallway. "What floor do you and David live on?" I asked.

"Eight," she replied.

I looked at her and said, "This is six."

I got her safely into her apartment and staggered back to the comfort of my own tenement. I looked forward to comparing hangovers with Merrill in the morning.

27

Easter in Slovenia

EASTER IS SUPPOSED TO BE one of the signs that spring has arrived, but it was still quite cold in Slovakia. Both of our schools gave us the week off to celebrate the Resurrection, and we decided that what Jesus would want most for both of us would be to take a trip to a warmer climate. Choices were limited. The only logical direction was southward. We wanted to go somewhere that was unique and that we were unlikely to go to again. That fact, plus Italy being expensive for two people living on Slovak Crowns, led us to look at Slovenia.

Slovenia is a part of the former Yugoslavia, which was a nation of six republics—Serbia, Croatia, Slovenia, Bosnia and Herzegovina, Macedonia, and Montenegro. The nation was formed following World War I, placing a variety of ethnicities with their own perceptions of national identity under one flag. By 1946, they even had their own dictator, Josip Broz Tito to hold them together. Tito died in 1980. It had been his authoritarian rule that was keeping all of these regions filled with people that had nationalistic sentiments from rising up. With the fall of the Berlin

Wall in 1989, the Domino Theory played itself out, but in reverse, and revolutions were happening across Eastern Europe, some bloody, and some bloodless. For Yugoslavia, it was the former.

In Yugoslavia, the various republics began seceding. Serbia, which had always been the dominant force in Yugoslavia retained the bulk of the military, and began invading its neighbors, in the name of protecting ethnic Serbs. Their leader, Slobodan Milosovic, was a modern-day Hitler. His generals oversaw the mass murder of men of other ethnicities and religions, and mass rapes of women by their soldiers in order to impregnate them with Serbian seed.

Slovenia fared far better in the war than its neighbors. A local explained to me over drinks how the Slovene part of the war played out.

"What do you think people do when they declare independence?" he asked.

"I don't know," I replied.

"Think," he said. "You have been forced to be a part of this nation for years that has nothing to do with who you are. Your lives are dominated by the Communists for fifty years. You had no rights. People were constantly spying on you. You could go to jail for just making a minor criticism of the government. Now you are free and have the chance to reclaim your real country and identity. What do you do?"

"Celebrate?" I asked.

"Exactly," he said. "And that is exactly what Croatia did, and now look at them. The Serb army has occupied over half of their country. We didn't do that. The day we declared independence we took over the military bases. When the Serbs invaded we were ready, and we fought back. After ten days, they decided it wasn't worth it. They would go fight the Croats. Not that many

Serbs live in Slovenia anyway, so they weren't as interested in us. And do you know what we did after the Serbs left?"

"Celebrated?"

"We were all drunk for a week!"

We decided not to tell our families we were going to go to a country in the former Yugoslavia. We had done our research, and we knew it was safe, but we also knew that everyone would worry if they knew we were visiting a country that had recently been involved in a civil war, not to mention the fact that the war continued to rage unabated nearby.

Leaving Banska Bystrica we took a bus to Bratislava. We arrived in the city at 4:00 a.m., and even in early April it was frigid, which was made worse by the fact that we were wearing somewhat lighter attire in preparation of warm weather. From Bratislava we traveled by train to Vienna. We had a layover, which allowed us to explore the city for a few hours. Everyone is supposed to experience a Viennese café at least once, and so we decided to visit one. We no doubt were already looking scruffy, so I am sure we looked out of place. After four months of living on Slovak Crowns, we were unprepared for Western prices. We ended up splitting a piece of cake and having two coffees that cost a total of six dollars. We had taken to measuring everything in terms of beer.

Merrill looked at me and said, "That was the same as eighteen beers back home!"

Let's hear it for being equated with reality. Remembering how angry Maja got when I suggested I understood what living under communism was like, I still couldn't help but feel some sympathy, if not outright empathy for Slovaks and how difficult it was for them to travel abroad. After living on Slovak Crowns for four months, a six-dollar café bill seemed like a fortune.

On the train to Ljubljana we met Sunny and Amy who were studying in Salzburg and were also on Easter break. They were joined by their father who had flown over from the United States to visit them. We talked for the entire train ride and decided to get rooms at the same hotel upon arrival.

As we exited the train station, we could immediately tell that spring had arrived in Slovenia. Not only was it warmer, but flowers were actually blooming. Slovakia was still slushy and grey, except for the sky which was brown from the coal that was being used to heat everyone's homes. As we looked around at everything blooming in vibrant shades of yellow, green, purple, pink, red, and white, it felt like we had moved from a black and white film to technicolor. Merrill noticed a tulip tree that was in full bloom, and I took a picture of him in front of it to have evidence that spring really did exist in Eastern Europe.

We changed money and the girls took the lead. They led us in a complete circle, back to the train station, but eventually we

Ljubljana, Slovenia

The author in Ljubljana

found the Hotel Park. We dumped our bags and went exploring. I had expected Slovenia to be a somewhat warmer version of Slovakia but couldn't have been more wrong. Perhaps it was because I had been in Slovakia for so long with relatively few breaks, but to me Slovenia seemed more Western than the West. There were Mercedes and BMWs on the roads. We had been used to Skodas, the national car of Czechoslovakia (the name actually translates to "it's a pity,"), East German Trabants, which were compared to papier-mâché, and Russian Ladas. One day Maros was driving me somewhere in his Lada and when he came to a stop sign all four doors flew open!

The city seemed to have everything for the weary Slovak vacationer. There was a modern downtown, but the buildings weren't filled with the Stalinist Towers we knew from Bratislava. They were stylish and visually appealing. The Old Town had been restored to its original beauty, and was filled with historical buildings, shops, restaurants, and bars, many along the river that ran through the historic district.

It was Merrill's birthday and we had dinner at an Italian restaurant that night to celebrate. Two bottles of wine and some lasagna later, we decided to walk through the main drag and decide where we should go for a drink. We stopped at two different bars. Then, as we walked along the cobblestoned street, a bar named Alex's caught our eye. Everyone inside began motioning for us to come inside so we obliged. It turned out that one of the people inside was having a birthday party. When we told them it was Merrill's birthday as well, Alex locked the door and declared it to be a private party. We didn't pay for another drink that night.

The next day we explored the city, visiting the various churches and museums. We also climbed up to the castle for an excellent panoramic view of Ljubljana. We were having a good time playing the role of tourists when we noticed a United Nations vehicle in the parking area for the castle. It was common for UN workers to

Merrill with the UN vehicle

come to Slovenia on their time off to escape the tragedy that was unfolding in the neighboring countries, and it reminded us that the situation was not so blissful just a very short distance away.

That afternoon Amy's boyfriend, Brent, arrived with Hayes. They were coming from Bled, a town in the Julian Alps. Brent told us the town was okay, but nothing incredible. We decided to see for ourselves.

28

No Blood in Bled

WE RENTED A ROOM AT a farmhouse that was just on the edge of town. We quickly exchanged money for a key with the two owners, who were leaving for an appointment. They did tell us that their grandmother would be home later if we had any questions. With that we were alone in a large house with no one else around. We were beginning to unpack when an air raid siren went off.

Merrill looked at me and said, "I don't like that sound." After a pause, he reiterated, "Let me just say this once more, I *really* don't like that sound."

I quickly moved away from the window, and not being able to think of anything else to do, we both spent a few minutes underneath our beds until the siren quit. Once it appeared all was quiet, we gathered our composure and walked to town. When we arrived there was a folk festival going on, and we asked one of the bystanders if he knew anything about the siren. He replied that they tested it every Saturday at noon. Our entire adrenalin rush had been for nothing. We were never in any danger at all.

What was merely okay to Brent and his friend was marvelous to both of us. Bled is a resort town, with a castle that tourists can hike to, as well as a church on an island in the center of a lake that is so photogenic, any amateur photographer can feel like a professional. We rented bikes and spent the day pedaling around the town.

Grandma stopped us as we were preparing to leave the next morning and told us we had to have breakfast. We explained that we had not paid for breakfast, but she didn't care, and said we had to eat. With that, she left and quickly returned with cold cuts, bread, butter, juice, and coffee. With full stomachs, we strapped on our backpacks and began the mile or so walk to the train station to begin our trip home.

Beautiful Bled, Slovenia

29

Grateful to Margaret in Graz

BACK IN LJUBLJANA WE BOARDED a train for Vienna. All of the compartments we passed initially were full, and then we came to one that had only a sole passenger. She was our age with dirty blonde hair and brown eyes. Both smitten, we asked if we could join her and she agreed.

Merrill, eager to pour on the old charm, instigated a conversation, and assuming our new travel companion was not a native English speaker, he began talking to her in very simple sentences which he thought would facilitate the conversation. He over-enunciated every syllable he spoke.

"Ljubljana is beautiful," he said, slowly and clearly.

"Yes, it is," she replied. "I come here often when I have time off.

"Where do you live?" Merrill inquired, in the same slow, methodical tone.

"I live in Graz, Austria. It's between Ljubljana and Vienna in southern Austria.

Slowly again, Merrill said, "You're English is very good."

"Thank you," she replied. "I'm from California, where are you from?"

So much for being smooth. Her name was Margaret, and she worked for the British Council teaching English. Train tickets allowed passengers the privilege of getting off between their starting and ending points without a penalty. Even though it was raining, she suggested that we join her for the day in Graz and she would show us the city.

We began our tour with a couple of beers and lunch, and then began exploring a very wet Graz, a charming and compact city. As we strolled and talked, Margaret said she wanted to show us the cathedral, named the Stadtpharrkirche. As we approached the altar, she asked us to examine the stained glass images and see if we could find anything unusual. We stared for several minutes, but didn't notice anything out of the ordinary, except for various religious images portrayed in vivid primary colors. She finally pointed to what we were supposed to notice. In one panel stood Hitler and Mussolini together. The overall window reflected images of Christ's tormentors. Hitler and Mussolini were added to the cast of characters following World War II.

We said our goodbyes to Margaret and headed farther north to Vienna. We would now be getting into the train station at about 1:00 a.m. and did not want to spend money for a half night in a hotel. Our plan was to stay in the train station until daylight, see a few sites that we might have missed during our layover on the way to Slovenia, and then get back on a night train to Banska Bystrica. Our plan worked perfectly for about two hours, when we were gruffly told to exit the building by a Viennese police officer. Apparently they cleared the South Train Station at about 3:00 a.m. each morning so that the custodial staff could clean.

Merrill and Margaret in Graz

We walked outside where it was drizzling and about forty degrees. There was absolutely nowhere we could think of to go. Then, I noticed a row of three telephone booths. We decided to take advantage of the only shelter that seemed to be available. Each of us took an end booth, and we stacked our backpacks in the middle one. I nodded in and out of sleep until the sun came up a couple of hours later. Before Morpheus overtook us though, we did take advantage of the setting and called our families to let them know where we were, where we had been, and that we were okay. No one back home was particularly happy about what we had done, but we were going to take the trip regardless, and this way they hadn't had to worry about our safety for a week.

We only spent a short amount of time in Vienna that day. I did not know about the concept of Easter Monday, but every traveler should be aware that Europeans take it seriously. Almost every place we tried to visit was closed. We were tired, dirty, cold, and wet from the perpetual Austrian drizzle. Sensing that we had both had enough adventures for one trip, we hopped a train back home to the creature comforts of our Sasovarian apartment.

30

God Killed Our Refrigerator

FOR ALMOST FOUR MONTHS WE had been using our apartment's balcony for a refrigerator. The situation was effectively a variation of binary code. If something was on the balcony it was frozen. If it was inside it wasn't. It wasn't the best system in the world, but it was working well enough. It probably would not have worked well enough had we not both been twenty-two years old and desperate to travel internationally. It is always strange to reflect and think about the luxuries you can live without when you are young. As spring approached though, Mother Nature, God, or the rules governing the climate killed our balcony of a refrigerator.

Starting in March, with the help of Maja as an interpreter, I had begun asking the Russian Bear director for a refrigerator. I consistently got the same response, which was they were very hard to come by in Slovakia, and also very expensive, but that he would try. By early April the situation had become untenable.

We weren't able to keep any dairy at the apartment, and it had reached the point that for any meal we wanted to eat at home, it was necessary to buy all of the ingredients just an hour or two beforehand.

I again asked Maja to serve as a translator, and asked her to translate the words "Delta is ready when I am." The Bear looked back at us quizzically and said he didn't understand.

I said, "Please translate, I am going to go back to my apartment, pack my bags, and get on an airplane to the United States if we don't have a refrigerator by the end of the week.

That evening when I came home from class, Merrill was stocking our brand new twenty-something-year-old refrigerator with groceries he had just purchased. "It's a Christmas miracle, just four months late!" he exclaimed.

31

You Get a Line and I'll Get a Pole

AS THE WEATHER BEGAN TO warm more opportunities to get out and explore—as the Slovaks liked to say—"The nature" presented themselves. A student in one of Maja's classes named Jaroslav asked me to join him and his wife at their cottage for a day of fishing that Sunday. The trip turned out to be more of a day of hiking and beer drinking rather than fishing. Jaroslav and his wife had caught all of the fish we could have ever wanted the day before.

His wife, Janka, was a marine biologist. I was curious about any health hazards relating to eating fish that were caught out of the Hron River. I knew that in Banska Bystrica itself there was effectively no life in the Hron, because of years of pollutants being pumped into the river by various companies. I had this image of any fish ever being discovered in the Hron as having two heads. She assured me that once you were north of the city, all of the water was clean and healthy, and that it was also the source of the drinking water for the city. In fact, Banska Bystrica was home to some of the healthiest and purest drinking water in Europe. I laughed at the memory of one young woman who was teaching with us in Banska Bystrica who called her parents and said she couldn't continue living in Slovakia because of the unhealthy drinking water. I later heard she had moved to Venice, which as everyone knows is home to some of the purest water in the world.

I am a wimp when it comes to hunting or fishing. I don't enjoy watching things die, and I certainly don't enjoy being a participant in their executions. Even when I have gone fishing, I feel bad for the fish flopping around waiting for the end to come. With that said, I have no problem eating whatever has been killed. I just prefer to not have to witness the dirty part of the process. Consequently, I didn't really mind not going fishing. The meal still ended up being a tad more gruesome than I expected.

Jarolslav fried each of us a fish in a large cast iron skillet. He put the whole fish in the pan and flipped them one time. Apparently, you knew they were done when the eyeballs popped halfway out. He then plopped the fish on a plate in front of me and said, "*Dobru chut*," which is the Slovak version of "*bon appetit*."

The meal was quite good; I was just unnerved by having the dead fish watch me as I pierced it with my knife and fork and shredded its flesh. As we finished our dinner, Janka took her fork, and jabbed it deep into the neck of the dead and now mutilated fish carcass. She pulled a brown thing out of the fish, and looked at me, her eyes gleaming with joy, and said, "Chrees, is the heert. Is my favorite part of the fish!" She then devoured the fish's heart. It was a fun, odd day.

32

Weekend in Donovaly

WE WERE NEARING THE END of the term, which meant that it was time for the State Language Exam. A dictation had to be read by one of the native English speakers. The Slovak students would write what the teacher said down on paper as best they could. I was popular with the students, but I was also their absolute last choice for the teacher to read the dictation because of my Southern accent. Compared to most people from Alabama my accent is quite light, but to a Slovak with three years of English language experience, it was a bit of a hurdle. The exam was on Saturday morning, and I was ultimately the teacher who was asked to do the reading. The teacher from Kansas, John with his newscaster voice, had already made plans to be out of town.

I was prepared for a quiet Friday night, but Dr. Moravic asked me if I would like to go to his cottage in the nearby town of Donovaly. Slovaks had been forced to relocate into suburban high-rise dwellings under communism. However, most had very small cottages—usually one room—that were on the outskirts of town that also came with a small amount of land. These places were used for family gardening, but they were also used for people to have a cheap getaway where they could have drinking parties. He also invited Maja, and three students. I explained that I had to give an oral exam the following morning, so I wouldn't be able to leave town. He countered that he would gladly drive me back and have me at the school in time for the testing. I told him it was too much trouble, and he explained that it was no trouble at all. A casual observation about Slovaks—they may have never been a global power, but on an individual basis they can definitely wear a person down until they are victorious. They can also flip a situation, so that it is almost impossible to turn them down without somehow hurting their feelings, which I never wanted to do. I acquiesced. We met at his office near Banska Bystrica's square, and he drove us in a small van to Donovaly, which was twenty minutes away, and located in the High Fatras mountain range.

We arrived in Donovaly at about 7:00 p.m. The town was completely surrounded by mountains. Leading to the mountains were purple fields colored by thousands and thousands of Crocus flowers that were seemingly planted everywhere. In the distance, toward a forested area we could see a group of about twenty roe deer.

Once we arrived at the cottage itself, I was quite surprised. I had been wondering how so many people could spend the weekend in a typical Slovak cottage based on the ones I had visited previously. This was not a typical Slovak cottage. It slept seventeen and had three stories, including a bar in the basement. If there was a negative it was that there was no shower, so we would be smelly little naturalists by the end of our weekend trip. I decided that based on what I had already seen, it was worth it for the scenery and the company.

A night—or in this case a weekend—at a Slovak's cottage involves drinking on a dangerous scale. Usually, there is a pot of goulash on the stove, which is a hearty fare for the surprise that awaits participants' livers. There were two typical snacks that were put out at these events. The first was *slanina,* which the Slovaks refer to as bacon in translation. It was actually fatback. It was incredibly slimy, and the first time Merrill and I were offered it, we thought it was raw and wondered how the entire nation had avoided developing trichinosis. It is actually smoked, and there is nothing that can be said about smoked fat other than it is slimy, although under heightened circumstances it does begin to taste good. The other snack was diced onions. Everyone would go back and forth between the two basic food groups as the night wore on, eating more and more fatback and onions, while getting increasingly inebriated and flatulent. If someone needed more substantive food, there was goulash on the stove.

The bottles lined up on the table were more than enough for the six of us. There were several bottles of red wine—which were Maja's and my preference—three bottles of vodka, and a bottle of slivovitz. We talked, drank, ate onions and fatback, and were generally merry until about 3:00 a.m. when we went to bed. Two hours later, Dr. Moravic—Jan by this point—woke me up with considerable effort. I brushed my teeth, but I feared that I would have onion breath for some time to come. With my breath being cleansed of the evening's sins as best as possible, we were off to Banska Bystrica. I had been asked to be at the school at 7:00 a.m. in order to meet with all of the teachers and the principal before the exam that would follow in an hour.

We arrived in plenty of time, and although I was a tad wobbly, all things considered I was in fairly good shape. I stepped out of the elevator and walked to the director's office, and there he was in all his Russian bearishness. Several other teachers were there as well, all of them holding a combination of sherry glasses, liqueur glasses, and for the ones who were late to the party—shot glasses. Ah, morning at a Slovak school!

The bear lumbered over to me and said, "Vodka ... cognac?"

I tried to politely decline but was immediately told by many of the teachers in the room that it would be rude to refuse. Why not, I thought to myself. Most of my liver should still be functional after this six-month adventure.

"Vodka," I said.

He looked at me, and said, "Vodka and cognac," and handed me two shot glasses. It was 7:00 a.m., and I hadn't had a drink in at least four hours. Everyone watched to make sure that I really did drink both shots. Now I was ready to give a test!

Once in the classroom, I read the dictation slowly and clearly, and made sure to repeat as many times as possible. The students may have ultimately benefited somewhat by having their marginally soused Alabama teacher being the one delivering the dictation. Someone else probably would not have read as slowly or given so many second chances. Regardless, everyone felt good about the test when it was over, and with that mission accomplished I walked to Jan's office at the Polyclinic.

Jan and Maja were both waiting for me in his office on the 4th floor of the building. He handed me a cup of coffee and told me we were going hiking that afternoon to the top of Zvolen Peak, which rose to 1,407 meters. He looked at me—from what I could tell he had to be checking to see what condition my condition was in—and reached into a cabinet and handed me a pill.

"You need to take a vitamin," Jan told me.

I followed the doctor's orders. Maybe it was a vitamin, and maybe it was something else, but with little sleep, and more alcohol in me than I can conceive of imbibing today, I made it to the top of the mountain with no difficulty.

33

Fast Budapest

If Merrill and I had a city that served as our travel nemesis, it was Krakow, Poland. It was only about four hours to our north. We had to change trains in Zilina, Slovakia, and it was a straight shot from there. I had wanted to see Krakow since childhood. One of my favorite picture books had been the vividly illustrated *The Magician of Krakow*. I was curious to see the city and also learn how it compared to the illustrations in the book. I knew the Magician wouldn't be there. He ended up living on the moon at the story's end.

We were planning to take a train out of the Banska Bystrica train station at 11:57 at night. This would be our third attempt trying to visit Krakow. We somehow arrived at the train station at 11:58 p.m. A note about Slovak trains—they are not necessarily fast, but they are punctual. It was midnight in a Slovak train station and we both had heavy backpacks strapped to us and nowhere to go.

Merrill looked at me and said, "What do you want to do?"

I looked up at the schedule, and noticed a train was leaving for Budapest in about a half hour. I turned to him and said, "I have never been to Budapest."

Merrill's response was, "Me neither!" We bought two tickets immediately, and soon we were moving, just in the opposite direction that we had intended.

Budapest, Hungary, might win the competition for the world's most beautiful parliament building. It is in the Gothic Revival style, with an impressive dome in the center that is representative of the Renaissance Revival style. It sits astride the Danube River, and dominates everything around it. The many bridges linking Buda and Pest—it was originally two cities—give Budapest a romantic charm. We stayed in a youth hostel that was in a converted castle that overlooked the city. As hostels go, it wasn't that great, but it would have been impossible to find a place with a better view. There were probably twenty or thirty beds per room, but it was a place to sleep. I always felt safe in hostels. Travelers who are backpacking have a sort of "honor among thieves" mentality. Even though we were all strangers, in general, we knew no one was likely to mess with us or our stuff.

Ethnic divisions seemed to be common in Eastern Europe. We always thought of it more as people joking about their neighbors. In Alabama, for instance, the standard joke is "thank God for Mississippi." Slovaks often had something negative to say about the Czechs, who they saw as their equals and just got lucky by having Prague, meaning they more or less believed the Czechs were uppity. The Czechs saw the Slovaks as effectively their country cousins. Slovaks also were not fond of the Austrians, who they viewed as rich and a former conqueror. The Ukrainians, we were told, were dangerous. "It is like visiting the Wild West," one Slovak told me. Coming from the land of Polish jokes, I was surprised that everyone I met admired the Poles,

The parliament building in Budapest

who they viewed as intelligent. They also believed the Poles understood the concepts of capitalism better than other people in the region. Everyone hated the Magyars, which is the ethnic term for Hungarians. They had dominated the entire region at one point or another.

The Magyars in some ways defeated me as well. The Hungarian language is like no other in central Europe. Instead of being a Slavic language—which can be adjusted to once a person gets used to words with five or six consonants in a row—I found Hungarian to be largely indecipherable. To some extent, we were dependent on signs with English translations, which were few and far between in 1993.

We ended up finding some places where translations were not necessary. I have always been a believer in eating local cuisines wherever I am. I can remember being in Venice with a group in 1989, and the moment we arrived, all of the American

The Budapest Bastion

students somehow found a Wendy's fast food restaurant. I was horrified, thinking about all of the amazing restaurants within a few footsteps. We had only been walking around Budapest for a short time when we noticed a Kentucky Fried Chicken. I don't believe I had ever been into one of their franchises before 1993.

I hadn't had fried chicken since early January, and, worried that Alabama might rescind my citizenship, it seemed like an obligatory stop. We had fried chicken, mashed potatoes, and black-eyed peas. It was glorious.

As it turned out, American fast food had arrived in Budapest in serious force. There was also a Dairy Queen, where I got to have my first real hamburger in months. The Slovaks, and most everyone else in central Europe, have hamburgers, but they make them with ground pork. Merrill once asked a Slovak butcher if he could pay him to grind some beef for him.

"No," said the butcher.

"Why not?" asked Merrill.

"I would have to clean the grinder after running beef through it before I could go back to grinding pork," was the reply. That certainly made us feel good about the sanitation standards in area butcher shops!

From there it was onward to Dunkin' Donuts. We couldn't believe our eyes! The irony, of course, was that the Slovak pastries were far better than anything Dunkin' Donuts could ever hope to create, but we were having a bit of homesickness cured that we didn't really realize we had been experiencing. The Hungarians didn't quite understand American gluttony. I had never purchased doughnuts in quantities fewer than a dozen. They were selling them individually. We went back five or six times, and when we left it wasn't because we couldn't have eaten more, but because we knew everyone was looking at us like we were more than a tad odd.

That night we found a jazz bar that had a good band. We listened to music and drank late into the night. As we tried to find our way from the bar to the road that led to the hostel, we got lost and found ourselves going in circles. Tired, we finally sat down on a bench to rest. When I looked up I noticed a street sign. We were on Atilla Street. Once again, I had the feeling of being a stranger in a strange land.

34

Life in Slovakia

I ADAPTED QUICKLY TO LIVING in Slovakia, and perhaps more so than some of the other American teachers. As I have written, the food was not as much of a culture shock to me as to some other people. From an American perspective, the difficulty many people faced was the lack of choices of food (and everything else) that we were collectively accustomed to in the United States. Today, I live in a relatively small town in Alabama, but if I want to go out to dinner, I have options that range from restaurants offering barbeque to Japanese to Mexican to Mongolian to Indian. Plus, there are two fine dining options. In Banska Bystrica there were a lot of restaurants serving similar things, plus one pizza restaurant, and two Asian restaurants run by North Vietnamese immigrants.

The grocery stores had one type of whatever they were selling, when they had that. Our apartment was on a good day minimalistic. What I learned from all of this about myself was that I am no doubt materialistic. I only have to look around my house today to realize that. However, I am not as dependent on physical things as I might have thought before making this trip as I would have believed beforehand. Traveling to other places, meeting new people, and getting into adventures far outweighed—for me—the luxuries of the United States. Perhaps that is easy to say when you know you get to return home in a half year.

Slovaks were fastidious when it came to their clothing. As I got to know people well enough to go into their homes, I noticed everything was either hung up in a closet, or neatly folded and put away. Nothing was ever slung over a chair, as I have always been wont to do. If I took off a coat or jacket and tried to drape it over something while visiting a Slovak friend, a hanger would quickly appear. I came to realize that no one had wardrobes as extensive as what I was used to as an American. The people I met certainly had enough clothes for their daily lives, but not a surplus, and they needed to take care of them and make them last.

While walking through the square in Banska Bystrica one day with Maja a man in a nice suit walked past us. She made a "tsk, tsk" noise.

"What's up?" I asked.

"Most men," she replied, "will only have one suit like that in their lives."

I thought about my mother taking me to Brooks Brothers when I was six or seven to be measured for a sport coat. I decided to remain quiet.

Maja was often fascinated with some of the supplies that I brought from home. I had known that I would be making this trip for some time and had read widely on what to expect in terms of not so much deprivations, but inconveniences. One of the items I packed was a large box of Ziploc bags. One day I brought something to her in in a Ziploc, and she was fascinated. I don't think I could have cured a disease and impressed her as much as I did by giving her that little plastic baggie. Several weeks later, I paid her a visit, and while in the kitchen I noticed the Ziploc bag, which had been repeatedly washed and reused by this point.

Telephones were scarce, only one out of every four residents had one. The free flow of information had not been particularly encouraged by the previous regime. In forcing the populous to use the post office for most foreign calls, it was possible for the government to keep tabs on anything subversive that might be said with the help of the post office babushka's intrusive ear. On several occasions, Americans had the operator at the post office say something that made it clear they were listening to our conversations.

It is also worth considering what could be viewed as subversive. Vaclav Havel, the one-time dissident, and eventual president of the Czech Republic was known for creating absurdist poetry. One of his poems that angered state officials was titled Communist Progress. All the poem consisted of were the words Communist Progress over and over again, and this was put on paper in the shape of a circle. I have doubts that my inner smart ass would have allowed me to stay out of jail during the Communist era.

The Slovaks did receive one inheritance from the Soviets when they pulled out of Eastern Europe. They got an air force that included twenty-one MIG fighter jets. *Top Gun* with Tom Cruise had been a hugely popular movie just a few years earlier, and it was bizarre to see that particular model of fighter flying overhead. They could only fly east to west though. Slovakia is a very narrow country, and if the planes had flown north or south, the risk was too great that they would accidentally invade Poland or Hungary when they broke the sound barrier.

The ratio of dentists to citizens was one to ten in 1993 Slovakia. Dental care, much less orthodontic care was at best, weak. I am sensitive to this, because I had such terrible teeth as a child. I could have likely eaten corn on the cob through a chain link fence. I just had the good fortune of being able to have braces on my teeth. If someone had a cavity, the most common solution was to pull the tooth. Dentists—and everyone else—had effectively worked for the state. The state valued things that made it stronger and saved it money. A dental filling would not strengthen the state, and pulling a tooth would save money compared to taking the time for a filling or cap.

An American woman who had been in Slovakia for longer than me related a story about her adventures in dental care. She mentioned to a Slovak friend that she had a toothache and needed to find a dentist. The person told her that he knew a dentist, but that she would probably want to go to Prague like most of the other Americans when they had trouble with their teeth.

"Why would I want to go to Prague when I could just go to a dentist here?" she asked.

"The Americans just do," he replied. "Ees much more expensive too. In Prague they use something called the Novocain."

If dentists were scarce, dermatologists were non-existent. At first when I saw people on the street, I would think, there are some moley people here. I came to realize that the state had no interest in someone having a mole removed, and consequently there were no dermatologists. When I returned a few years later, I noticed that a lot of the people on the street had bandages on their faces. It took me a few minutes to connect the dots, but then I realized that the scope of medical practices had increased in Slovakia.

35

Krakow and Auschwitz

WE DID FINALLY MAKE IT to Krakow. It was the fourth attempt, but we got there. Upon arrival, we found someone who was offering to rent out his apartment to us for a few days. The Polish Zloty had collapsed, and Poland was in bad economic shape at the time. The economy had entered a period of hyper-inflation. When we changed money the person at the exchange booth handed us a stack of paper money like we had never seen before. To make it more interesting, the notes in some cases were for 50K and 100K Zloty, making mental currency conversions almost impossible.

Krakow is home to an ancient university, a beautiful old town dating to the Middle Ages, a city wall, and multiple museums and churches. It is also the city where John Paul II resided when he was a bishop. It is the only city in Europe where I felt slightly uncomfortable visiting the churches. When we entered any church regardless the time of day, there were several people inside praying, which is obviously not unusual. I kept randomly encountering scenes, though, where people were reciting the rosary. They were rocking back and forth, and were in tears. I didn't know what sort of dilemma these people were experiencing, but it made me feel that at least in this city, I wouldn't view churches as tourist sites.

We had been told that the outdoor market in Krakow was excellent, so we made a point of visiting. I had started the tradition of purchasing a chess set when we would visit a country. I started doing this in Prague and had already collected three. There were unbelievably beautiful sets available throughout the market that were large in scale and inexpensive. I bought two, both supposedly with all of the pieces hand carved, something that I doubt is true, but regardless, I am still incredibly fond of both sets.

Souvenir shopping wasn't something we ever really did much in Slovakia, and we were low on presents to take home to our families. We both bought handmade wool sweaters for our mothers that we thought were appealing, but also representative of the area we had been visiting, since they were made by locals. *Be appreciative, Mom,* I thought to myself, *a babushka toiled for hours making this for you.*

Moving onward we also found a variety of hand carved woodworks, such as plates, and boxes with engravings on them that would serve as good presents. It was then that Merrill stumbled onto the music section. We had listened to the cassettes we brought enough times that we had effectively memorized the words to every song in our collections. There was a big black market in Poland for pirated music, that was then sold cheaply at markets such as the one we were in. Merrill quickly scooped up several CDs, including one by Van Halen.

We went to an outdoor restaurant that night and sampled the local beer. On the label were two goats who were standing on their back legs and having what looked to be an affable conversation. It was a perfect night to be sitting outside. The sky was clear, the temperature was mild, and people were milling about between the different bars and restaurants, or just strolling around the square. It was easy to imagine what it must have been like to live during the Medieval period, had the Medieval period had electricity and running water. I ordered a pizza with ham and pineapples to go with the beer that night—a Hawaiian pizza. I had never had one before but couldn't think of a more bizarre setting than this ancient Polish city to try one for the first time.

Merrill was quite keen to visit Auschwitz. I did not particularly want to go. In hindsight, it would have been a mistake not to go see a site as important to world history as Auschwitz, but my BA was in history, and I had seen quite a lot of original and grim footage of what the camps were like. I had also been to Dachau, which gave me an even more concrete idea of what to expect at Auschwitz. We did ultimately decide to make the day trip to visit the camp though, which is about an hour's bus ride from Krakow..

At the entrance of Auschwitz is a large sign that reads "*Arbeit Macht Frei,*" which translates in English to "Work Makes One Free." The camp was literally a factory of death and was responsible for approximately 1.5 million of the Jews, Gypsies, and political dissidents who were killed in World War II. The Nazis were remarkably efficient. Of the roughly 460,000 Jews Hungary sent to Auschwitz, 438,000 were murdered.

It is hard for the human mind to process what happened at Auschwitz. Today, the camp is both a museum and a memorial to those who lost their lives there. In order to help visitors come to better understand the human toll there are rooms that are glassed in with personal affects that were found after the war. One room has shoes, shaving brushes, tooth brushes, and other toiletries. These are piled in a classroom-sized space four or five feet high. The visual that is impossible to forget though, is a similarly sized room that is filled with nothing but human hair. It is likely impossible ever to comprehend the level of horror and suffering that took place at Auschwitz, but for me, that one room came as close to making me understand what happened there as I possibly ever could.

The bus ride back to Krakow was fairly quiet. We returned to Banska Bystrica the following day.

36

The End Is Near, Run for the Hills

As we entered May, my time in Slovakia was drawing ever closer to a close. Outdoor adventures became near-daily routine. All of the Americans were thrilled that warmer weather had arrived, and there was plenty of free time to explore since all of us were working about twenty-four hours per week. I spent much of this time hiking and cooking out with Merrill, David, and Marie.

With hills surrounding the entire city, it was easy for us to take a new hike or create a variation on an old one whenever we wanted. The climb up was always harder because we had supplies to carry. In book bags, we toted sausages to cook, matches to start a fire, a loaf of bread, butter, several bottles of red wine, at least one bottle of vodka, and if David was so inclined, a bottle of Zwack. It is important to keep in mind that we were going to be gone all afternoon.

Once we reached our destination, or were tired of walking (whichever came first), we found a good spot, and built a fire.

I had never been exposed to camping of any kind in my life. I didn't tell any of my compatriots this, but instead paid close attention to everything they did. Once the fire was going, we found sticks and took out our handy Swiss Army Knives and began whittling one end of each stick so that it was pointed. We would then slice both ends of the sausages, pierce them with the sticks and hold them over the fire until they were cooked. They would curl up some from the heat, and Merrill liked to call them "meat stars." They were delicious although you didn't want to chew them too aggressively. I think the Slovaks were a little sloppy in the slaughtering process. There always tended to be a good sized bone in at least one of the sausages. It is a wonder we didn't all come back as a bunch of snaggle-pusses, but if we had lost a tooth or two, I still think it would have been worth it.

Early one evening, we had been up in the hills for several hours. The sun was going down, and Banska Bystrica, with its medieval clock and cathedral towers rising up from the valley below made it feel like we had traveled not just to another place, but another time. We each had at least a liter of red wine in us, and the vodka was more or less gone. We knew it was time to go, but we continued to linger because the view was so lovely. We realized that suddenly a storm was quickly developing when lightning bolts started shooting from the low-hanging clouds above us. Because we were on a hilltop, we felt like we were more or less in the middle of the lightening-filled clouds, rather than below them. There was enough electricity in the air that all of us could feel the hair on our heads and arms rising up.

We quickly gathered up our empty bottles. The men honored the ages long tradition of pissing on the campfire to make sure it was out. The fire had actually died out a good while earlier, but pissing on the fire just always seemed like the thing to do.

We then began a hasty descent back down to the city. By this point, the wind had picked up as well, and the rain was starting. We ran, slid, and careened our way down the hill, and returned to our apartments with a few scrapes, but feeling no particular pain.

37

Dolny Kubin

CARY MAY HAVE GOTTEN ONE of the more unique living situations of any of the American lectors. Education for Democracy placed him in a culinary school in Dolny Kubin. He lived in a vast old building that housed eighteen separate, fully equipped kitchens. Among the devices they were stocked with were blenders. He offered to host a weekend getaway for all of the Americans and suggested that each guest should bring some sort of fruit to make daiquiris, and of course, food to eat. Similar to our Mexican party, it seemed bizarre to think about a daiquiri party in central Slovakia!

Merrill and I showed up with a watermelon. I can't remember how he found it. The Slovaks did not really have the concept of watermelons as Americans know them. They would harvest them early and make a remarkably good tasting soup from them. We would later refer to this as the "weekend of debauchery." We hiked and cooked sausages over fires, ate Slovak dishes at a nearby restaurant, drank a lot of things that probably should never have been created, and repeatedly played Jenga. I am still not sure how that game ended up in the Middle-of-Nowhere, Slovakia. In between the frivolity, it was good to see many of the Americans who had been scattered across Slovakia for one last time.

38

The Farewell Tour

SAYING GOODBYE TO PEOPLE WAS a long process in Slovakia. Samuel and Susan invited me for a farewell dinner. Somehow, Samuel had acquired a bottle of Johnny Walker scotch, which he insisted on our starting the meal by taking a couple of shots.

When we sat down for dinner, we began with a soup that tended to be typical of a first course in Slovakia. It was very brothy and had perhaps nine strings of spaghetti and three slices of carrots. The Slovaks were adept at scooping out one carrot slice per person, as well as serving an equal number of the meager noodles for each person. All of the food that I had was so remarkably good, it took me a long time to understand why they consistently ate this less-than-impressive creation. I later realized the answer was simple. It would put some food in your stomach, so that you either didn't overeat, or if you were low on funds for food—as was likely the case at various points in Slovak history—you weren't hungry after a meager meal.

This meal would not be meager. Susan always proved to be an excellent cook, and this evening she had made a chicken dish. I complimented her on how good the chicken tasted. She looked perplexed.

"No, Chrees, no. Ees not chicken."

She then started thumbing through an English-Slovak dictionary. After several minutes she said, "Cock. You are eating cock." It looked like I would get to perform one last act as an English teacher for the Vizi family.

Before I left, Susan presented me with a pink porcelain dish that had been hand painted in Slovakia. I have no doubt that I should have been the one giving them a present. By inviting me into their home, I learned so much about Slovak culture that I would have otherwise never known.

39

All Good Things Must Come to an End

I RETURNED HOME ON JUNE 24, 1993. I did not want to go home, but there were several reasons to go back. My grandmother was eighty-five and was going to have surgery within the next month. At that age, I realized I might never have the chance to see her again. Also, if I was going to get a job as a teacher, I needed to go home, so I could begin interviewing for positions for the fall.

I was incredibly jealous of my compatriots who had made the decision to stay in Slovakia for another year, although their lives and addresses would be changing as well. Merrill would continue as an English teacher for a little while, but later moved into a role as a pharmaceutical representative for a company named Biotika. David and Marie moved to Bratislava where they continued their Slovak experience in a more urban setting.

We had a farewell party two nights before my flight home. I wanted to leave a day early to catch my flight out of Vienna.

Doing so would eliminate the chance of me missing a train or having some other type of delay. Many of my students, Josef and Lucy, Susan and Samuel, Maja, as well as a crowd from the Gastro Centrum were there. It was a fun if not wistful night. As I stood on our balcony and looked out at the evening sky, it suddenly dawned on me that I could see the moon. Because of a combination of the clouds, and the pollution caused by coal heating that was used to stave off the frigid winter, the moon had not been that common a sight. Also, it was just so cold during the winter, I probably wasn't thinking too much about stargazing. As I stared at the beautiful moon from what was formerly our refrigerator, I turned to Merrill.

"Would you take a look at that?"

"What?"

"There's a moon over Sasova."

EPILOGUE

I **WAS FORTUNATE ENOUGH TO** go to Slovakia during a time of great optimism. The Soviet Union was an "evil empire" of the past, and democracies were emerging throughout the Eastern Bloc nations. These nations were not just emerging as democracies, but also embracing their true histories, cultures, and national identities, so there was a somewhat romantic angle to the types of individuals they wanted to lead them. They were in search of people who were either national heroes for their participating in liberating their countries from the Soviets, or they were individuals who were in some way tied to the cultural history of the nation. In the Czech Republic, the people elected Vaclav Havel, the absurdist playwright-turned political dissident as president. In Poland, the long-time political activist Lech Walesa became the leader. Vytautus Landsbergis, Lithuania's choice for a leader, was a music professor before entering politics. In Vladimir Meciar, the Slovaks more or less elected someone who was similar to a leader they might have had during the Cold War. He definitely had some dictatorial tendencies. Their path toward having a romantic hero was dashed either by fate or murder.

Alexander Dubcek was the Communist leader during the 1968 Prague Spring. Born in the Slovak half of Czechoslovakia, he believed that it was possible to have what he referred to as "communism with a human face," and began allowing more freedoms for the Czechoslovak people. In response to this push for openness and freedom, the Warsaw Pact nations, at the command of their puppet masters in Moscow, invaded the country and there were quickly tanks on Wenceslas Square. Dubcek was expelled from the Communist Party in 1970, began working for the Forestry Service and lived in Bratislava. He continued to be viewed as a positive figure though, particularly in Slovakia. He was the second person to win the Sakharov Prize for Freedom of Thought, and soon afterwards received an honorary doctorate from the University of Bologna.

It was widely believed that Dubcek would be elected the first leader of the newly formed Slovak state. This was not to be the case though, as he was killed in a car accident on November 7th, 1992. He missed seeing an independent Slovakia by only a few weeks. It was widely rumored while I was in Slovakia that his death was really a political assassination. This was never proven, but regardless, instead of a romantic leader who tried to stand up to the Soviets, the Slovaks got Vladimir Meciar, who was a nationalist known for corruption and cronyism.

Similar to a person, within the context of a national mindset, you can only lose your virginity once. The welcome I received in Slovakia in 1993, as well as the attitudes and vibes I felt in Prague in 1991, would likely be impossible to replicate now. Americans were a new and shiny object of fascination for the Slovaks. Their understanding of capitalism was far too fragile to understand that it would be impossible to turn their country into a mini-United States overnight. I also am not convinced that it would have been good for Slovakia to have done so.

I returned to Slovakia in 1995, 1996 (to teach again for a half-year), and finally in 2007 for a brief visit following a fellowship in Germany. Although there is no way to quantify my beliefs on this topic, I believe the Slovaks are a far happier people than we are in the United States. Slovaks—and Europeans in general—are far less focused on their work lives than their personal lives. When I returned in 1996 to teach for a half-year, I was amazed at the amount of free time I had to go for walks in the surrounding hills and mountains, the willingness of people to go out for lunch, dinner, or drinks, and just the general relaxed atmosphere in society. As a teacher in the United States, we all seemed to be running in circles while trying to teach to meaningless objectives and filling out paperwork to prove we were teaching students content related to the meaningless objectives.

The entire time, our students' scores (the South and the rest of the United States) were among the worst in the developed world. Slovak students, in my experience, received a good education, but everyone had time for personal enjoyment. Furthermore, the American obsession of micromanaging every second of their children's daily schedule did not exist, which allowed for everyone to have their own lives. Teachers' lives in the United States are micromanaged almost as much as the students, leading to the entire educational experience in the United States far too open to comparisons to its penal system.

Something that I do lament is how difficult it would be today for a young person—or any person—to replicate the experiences that I had in 1993. Some of the countries that I visited are now regressing into the totalitarian regimes of yesteryear, most notably Hungary under Viktor Orban and Poland under Andrzej Duda. To the east, countries such as Belarus were never able to shake their authoritarian leader, and the eastern part of Ukraine has been left in a state of chaos through civil war and Russian annexation.

Slovakia, oddly enough, is showing promise. The nation that

does not have the word "city" in its language, only a few places qualify as big towns, and most people live in villages—little Slovakia, after flirting with authoritarianism, and organized crime infiltrating its government—has elected a president who may foretell a bright future for this nation of 5.5 million. After a journalist was assassinated for revealing links between government officials and the mafia, protests began and were followed by the election of Zuzana Caputova, a young and progressive leader who is a firm believer in liberal democracy. As we watch our own problems in the United States in 2021 and beyond, perhaps it will be the small nation of Slovakia who will become a positive example for the world of what a democracy should look like; something they learned in part, quite ironically, from the United States and Education for Democracy a quarter of a century ago.

AKNOWLEDGMENTS

IN WRITING ANY BOOK, THERE are so many people who assist in bringing the work out of the mind of the author and onto the printed page. Early on, I turned to a former student, Victoria Cubera, who had experience editing. She regularly proofed drafts of chapters and provided much needed encouragement. Merrill Bennett read an early draft of *Moon over Sasova* and also assisted me with remembering a variety of experiences from our time in Slovakia in 1993. My good friend, Dr. Tom Nadar, died unexpectedly in 2016, but he still came to the rescue when his brother, Don, gave me a stack of our correspondence that also included several letters from when I was living in Banska Bystrica.

Once the draft was complete, Liz Reed used her editorial skills actively to correct my passive voice. She and her husband Jim also published two chapters of *Moon over Sasova* in the *Birmingham Arts Journal*, which they edit. Dr. Kirk Curnutt, Chair of English at Troy University, provided me with extensive notes that helped me tell a better story. Kirk, Michelle Richmond, and Cassandra King also provided reviews of *Moon*, for which I am very grateful. Dr. Jeff Weddle of the University of Alabama's School of Library and Information Science was also an early reader and provided me with much encouragement. Jason Lockwood, who was the first of our merry band from Education for Democracy to publish a memoir about the experience read the manuscript and provided insight into navigating the publishing industry. When I needed a book cover, Ed Noriega, of Troy University's Graphic Design program, stepped in and created a design that was perfect and also something I would have never thought of on my own. Thank you so much, Ed. Finally, thank you to Amber Pittman. You could teach a graduate-level class on the finer points of Microsoft Office, and I thank you for all of your help not only on this project, but also when I was working on my dissertation (you accidentally got left off of the acknowledgements on that one).

Many thanks to all of you for being my Village.

ABOUT THE AUTHOR

CHRISTOPHER SHAFFER IS DEAN OF Library Services at Troy University. A former history teacher, he taught in Slovakia in the first months after it became an independent nation in 1993, and also returned there for another teaching stint in 1996. Lessons learned in Slovakia, as well as from travels throughout Eastern Europe influenced his work both as a teacher and a librarian. Shaffer currently resides in Enterprise, Alabama, with his wife Amber and their two dogs—"the Girls"—Dolly and Molly.

WWW.HELLGATEPRESS.COM

Made in the USA
Columbia, SC
09 December 2021

50868613R00098